PRAISE FOR FACTORY GIRLS

A person can learn not only a lot, but *everything*, about the world—about the unplumbed shadows and fate and salvation of the world—by living beside and *inside* the movements and metamorphoses—the spinning—of those most vulnerable to being forcibly lost within it. I learn a lot—I learn *everything*—by listening, for example, to Takako Arai. Her poetry, through these brilliant translations, is, in fact, the kind of altar-as-homage-as-storytelling I need, especially now and always: that of the acute and deeply compassionate choreography of counting and recounting (sometimes into dancing) the dead.

—Brandon Shimoda

Ghosts, people, factories, and creatures blow through each other like smoke rings in Takako Arai's startling poems. Her images are so vivid and vermicular, they all but crawl under the reader's skin. Again and again, Arai shuffles present, past and future into a borderless time where dreamlife and factory work (which smells of "machine oil, hair oil, and breast milk") merge into a mythic quotidian, and every event, with its understated political implications, "spins on and on to the end of time." Arai siphons language from every kind of diction and lights it on fire. This is a book no one forgets.

—Forrest Gander

FACTORY GIRLS

Selected Poems of
Takako Arai

Edited by
Jeffrey Angles

Translated by
Jeffrey Angles, Jen Crawford, Carol Hayes, Rina Kikuchi,
You Nakai, and Sawako Nakayasu

Action Books, Notre Dame, Indiana, 2019

Action Books
Joyelle McSweeney and Johannes Göransson, Editors
Katherine Hedeen, Associate Editor
Maxime Berclaz, Sebastian Bostwick, and Natasha Ali, 2018-2020 Editorial Assistants
PJ Lombardo, Jasmine Ortiz, and Valerie Vargas, 2019-2021 Editorial Assistants
Jeffrey Angles, Daniel Borzutzky, Don Mee Choi, Advisory Board
Andrew Shuta, Book Design

ISBN 978-0-900575-84-6
Library of Congress Control Number:2019948877

First Edition

We may be reached at Action Books, English Department, 233 Decio Hall, Notre
Dame, IN 46556. Or visit us online at actionbooks.org.

TABLE OF CONTENTS

IN THE FACTORY

WHEN THE MOON RISES

It is the night shift in an abandoned spinning factory
There is only a single light bulb here —
The spools of thread turn by themselves
Click goes the bobbins
Changed by the machines
A decade has already gone by
Since this place shut down
But when the moon rises, it begins to work
Its strange automation
They say that soon after the war
A factory worker's hair got tangled
In the machines, killing her
There are things that float here
But this is not the work of ghosts
No
In the factory
There are peculiar habits
That is what I mean
Peculiar habits remain here
An old lady who spun thread
For forty-four years here
Still licks her index finger and twists
Even on her deathbed
She cannot escape the gesture
That must be true in the netherworld too
Since threads are so infinitely thin
Gestures sink into the bodies
Of those who manipulate the machines
And possess them
Look
How the raw silk thread
Is pulled smoothly
From the factory woman's fingers
Then dances endlessly
The factory is that way too
The axle of the spinning wheel
Remembers

The molecules of steel
Hang their heads in the
Direction in which they spin
Then get caught up
Clanging emptily
When the moonlight pours in
It is not just the tide that grows full

Emptily
        Emptily
The spinning wheels spin
The threads swim
Through the abandoned factory

haunting)

JA

BOBBINS

Behind closed eyes, her pupils light up
Lines of varied bobbins in a row
Licking the tip of her index finger
She carries her gesture
To the end of each fiber
So the elderly woman spins the thread
Of rapture
Into her dying days   *repetition*

The towel that hung around her neck for so long
Is gone now
Trickling down the back of her ears
Crawling down the length of her body
The cotton futon beneath her absorbs
The drops of life
Even as it grows
Soaking wet

She spins the thread
This isn't a dream, not the far shore
If anything, the bed
Is the bottom of a river
A whirlpool of
Spinning bobbins
Bringing threads together
Several bobbins turning
In wonder, coming close to one another
Tiny, half-translucent fish
Migrating threads
Skimming the water's surface

I've grown as thin as a snake
The thin sheets of a calendar torn off, disappearing before your eyes
This is such a strange spinning factory
Workers nowhere to be seen
Already, I
Am a thread

Am a whirlpool
Stitching together the slight spaces between water and waves
Stitching together the slight spaces between circles and wheels
Stitching together the slight spaces between breath and time
While growing a little more
Transparent
With each suture

I spin the wheel
The threads spin the threads
Meanwhile, the fish —
Never blink their eyes

JA

WHEELS

A fire's coming! It'll be here soon!
A female snake kept warning us
It lived for ages in the storage space above the closet
We grew up hearing its voice
Each time we laid out the bedding
Eventually my sister and I could hardly stand it
We'd lie in wait anxiously, temples pounding
Tonight, it'll be here! Tonight's the night!
Did you extinguish it? Did you put it out?
Did you smother it? Are there any cracks for it to get in?
We lowered our eyes to check

The snake was one of the factory girls three generations ago
She was so beautiful she turned the heads of men passing by
But the man she loved cheated on her
She took methamphetamines so often
She couldn't leave the workers' lodgings
She started having visions
She started hallucinating about fire
A fire's coming! It'll be here soon!
Perhaps she wanted to feel a fire burn down there
There were only women in the factory
They poured water into her mouth from a teapot
She came to for a moment
One side of her face smiled
But her expression looked so forlorn
Her hairline raised in a peak
A fire's coming! Hot! Hot!
She steamed, went into convulsions, and died among nightmares
They say they gave her a funeral right there
Her brother didn't come for her ashes
Even the locks of hair her co-workers saved
Were stashed away in storage
The hair was what cried out to us
Every night

The fire in the kitchen range, the fire in the stove
The charcoal in the brazier, the cigarettes in the ashtray
The heater beneath the bath
The metal latch in the sliding door, the window key
When my sister and I grew too intent
We'd look at one and forget what came before
The snake cried out, *Look, it's a trap!* And we would start all over
A fire's coming! It'll be here soon!
We were compelled to crawl around the floor
Who knows how many times our eyes licked
The charcoal stoves at the feet of the women
In the spinning factory?

The voice terrified me, got under my skin
My older sister was pulling my leg
Imitating the factory girl
She turned off the bathroom light so it was pitch black
And would imitate it, *A fire's coming! It'll be here soon!*
She made me cry
I cried and clung to her as she teased me
She was just trying to scare me
But even so
In the slowly cooling steam
She'd eye me with a strange gleam
As if speaking the truth
A fire's coming! A fire's coming! It's coming! It's coming!
The factory's going to burn!
Her voice, the voice evoked the snake
And it came after me
It turned upon me and came after me
It got under our skin, swallowing
The two of us together, nude

We endured as we rolled up the bedding
But we always crawled out
And it lifted itself up
And the factory girl
Looked at the source of the fire with us
We slithered, slithered, slithered
The ceiling spit out dust

‹ 6 ›

The handles on the chest rattled
I don't get it! The more I look
The more fiery apparitions in the sparks
We checked too often to see if the fire was out
      If the gas opening on the kitchen range was out
          If the cigarette butts in the ashtrays were out
             If the embers smoldering in the hibachi were out
We would light them
         We set our eyes upon
      The ghostly flame
Me chasing my sister who was chasing the factory girl who was chasing my
      sister who was chasing me who was chasing
Me who was chasing me who was chasing the factory girl who was chasing
      my sister who was chasing…
We were mice, gasping, forming a huge whorl
We were house mice, our breasts shaking in fear
We can't catch you!
We called out to the sparks

The spinning wheels smile

We often lit fireworks by the ditch by the factory
We brought the brass candlestick from our family's Buddhist altar
Brought colored paper near the flame for our ancestors
The powder sucked it in
It choked a little
Then the flame
Sprang up
Turned, kicked the gravel
Trying to steal the ankles of us children
Reflected in the water
Exploded and
Scorched the straps of our sandals, at the same time
It got under our skin
The flame had no feet
Nor did the dead
It tried to swallow us
We were the ones being chased
We were the ones
      It was after

The spinning wheels smiled

There was a bright red quilt
Sewn from old underclothes
The factory girl wore beneath her kimono
When I snuggled into it
My face grew red
Wind passed through my throat
Snuggle further down and
The setting sun shone, flashing
The thick snake started slithering
From the storage closet
Coming for the two little mice
Its eyes clear, the color of flame

     Flaring
              The flame
        Would crawl closer

Things were on fire
        The factory girl, her hair had come lose
              And had become heat shimmers
Things were on fire
        My sister stuck out her tongue
              From behind buck teeth
I stood
        On the edge of the ditch
The flame
        Burning my ankles

The spinning wheels turn. Turn in the hot wind. Turn with the hot hands of the flames. Turn intently. Turn like a coiled snake. Turn as they stare at fate. The spinning factory is a wheel of flame. It turns, swallowing a whirlpool of fire. It spins on and on to the end of the world. It spins on and on to the end of time.

It spins

It spins its bright red thread

JA

repetitive motions

BEDS AND LOOMS

My job as an operator was to call them out
An inexperienced girl like me
Pick up the receiver, run to the factory floor
And among the noise of looms—*clackity-clack, clackity-clack*
Stand up straight and shout into the women's ears
"Sat-chan, telephone!"

The call that day was for Yai-chan
                    I dashed through the places
            Where we punch the cards for the looms
Where we prepare the threads for the warp
Where we spin the thread, I saw a pornographic picture on the calendar
Like in a public path, breasts exposed
In a factory where all but the two loom fix-it men were women
They let the real thing spill over as well
When a baby cries, you've got to let them feed
The women working in the factory
Put their children on their back, carried them to the cribs
They saved their money
Machine oil, hair oil, and breast milk—
Those were the scents of the factory
I hated them, didn't want to breathe them in
Baby beds and power looms,
Baby beds plus power looms, baby beds as power looms
Clackity-clack, clackity-clack, clackity-clack, clackity-clack

The call was for Yai-chan
She had a reputation as a weaver
To finish weaving a bright red robe for a priest
You need good hands, good eyes, a good mind, a good vagina
It won't work if she doesn't, if she's not a woman among women
The woman manager would always say
                            Those priests never know women
                    It's not Buddhist recitations that let
            Them reach Nirvana
        It's our woman weavers
    It's the robes against their skin that calm their desires

Yai-chan's hand is the oar, rowing a small boat on the River of Three Hells
The gold-threaded brocade (four hundred thousand yen per meter)
Worn by the abbot of the high temple
Supported
The life of the factory
All twenty-two workers, their husband's liquor
Their mother-in-law's incense
Their sons' excursions at school

Yai-chan also had a child
With the delivery boy from the noodle shop
He kept his wife in the country a secret
Their relationship broke off, like noodles cooked to mush
In the stewing stomach of her anger
She gave the baby to her older sister and her husband
So that's why
Even though she was past thirty and her breasts were swollen
Not a single drop came out, nipples bound up tight
That's why the pornographic picture in the woman's factory by the
Baby beds and power looms, baby beds plus power looms, baby beds as
        power looms
Was an overripe icon of Yai-chan, she who had no one to give her milk
The woman manager would say,
                    "The worries that cause her to crease her brow
            Are what make her work late into the night
        Are what make her a woman among women
    We put our hands together and thank her"
Not a very considerate thing to say

My job was to call them out

Yai-chan was in the far back
If the caller got impatient and hung up
We had to pay to call them back so factory accounts determined my speed
I ran, I ran
                    I ran as fast as I could
Where we stored the thread, piled with spools
I noticed something, something flat
Clackity-clack, clackity-clack, the machines were moving by themselves
She wasn't there

The Maria-Kannon of the Weaving Factory wasn't there
She wasn't standing there
She was asleep, she was in bed
She'd hauled in a double bed!
              Yai-chan had been doing it
              During the lunch breaks with Shō-yan who fixed the looms!
Femurs before her sacred gate
Must have *creeeeeeaked*

              As they opened

                             (Who can say a baby bed was acceptable
                        But a double bed was not?
                   The factory worshipped her skill
              If in this woman among women
         We had a secret buddha
    Who had the right to say
She shouldn't open her shrine?

religion = sexuality

Her loom weaves the robes
Clackity-clack, clackity-clack
Phoenixes in pure gold thread
              Unfold line
              By line
Combs falling forth like plumes, claws sharpening
Dancing up
In the patterns on the back and sleeves of the priest's satin robes
The open eyes of the cloud dragon, long whiskers of the rising dragon, scales
         covering the mystic dragon
Danced down
To the birthplace of the thread
Where they intertwined
With the thread
To breathe in the sweat of the rustling sheets
From the double bed found there
Dragons, phoenixes, and lip-licking priests

Clackity-clack, clackity-clack, clackity-clack, clackity-clack
Double bed is a power loom, double bed as a power loom,
         double bed with a power loom
The woman manager

Foamed at the mouth in anger and
To this day still recites the Heart Sutra
Before the shrine of her ancestors

Clackity-clack, clackity-clack, clackity-clack, clackity-clack ~ onomatopoeia
Form itself is emptiness, Emptiness itself is form
Sex itself is emptiness, Emptiness itself is sex

Call them out

Be called out

(We women are called out

JA

NYLON SCARF

The weaving girls lived there
Played with me, tied cake ribbons into my hair
So much younger than mother
They stiffened when I threw my arms around them
They didn't stick to me
Though their breasts were soft
Clamoring like light falling through trees, there was an opening
Yeah, that—
Embarrassing, when I think of it now
When a child touches them
Pale nipples tighten
It tickled… Tickled me too
        So that's why I, still a little girl,
Would make a point to take them in my arms

On the wall of their lodgings
A girl with big, made-up eyes and flipped-out curls, a man in profile
        wearing a scarf
Magazine cutouts plastered the whole place
In the sharp scent of hairspray
The weaving girls made themselves up to look nice
Put the make-up on thick, like girls who trade their affections for cash
The girls competed
Stared into the mirror
Even when brushing their cheeks against a child
They felt it
Embarrassment, that is
They're closed in, turn on the factory lights
And they shake with the roar
That is
They look just like those who lean
Against the wall of a noisy disco
I get it now
Why they stayed so long in the factory

        I got in together
        One evening with Mat-chan

We borrowed the bathtub from the factory head's wife
She scrubbed me, my back, and my head
Called me her little kewpie doll
Made me stand up, covered in bubbles, and smiled
Then we submerged ourselves
To our necks, counted to fifty
Something changed
Her eye color
So quickly—*And go!*
She started to scoop out goldfish
No
None were there, of course
Mat-chan
Spread a thin towel outside the tub
And meekly
Began to scoop out
The body hair swimming in the tub
Kids don't need to help, she said
Over and over
She scooped them out
Even when I said there weren't any more
Splash, splash—Sopping, soaking wet
Dripped
Splash, splash—Sopping, soaking wet
How did we
Climb out of the bath?
How much did our warm bodies cool?
I don't remember
Was Mat-chan's name
Really Machiko? Or Matsuko perhaps?
I don't remember

When the girls left the lodgings
The factory owner's wife gave them a silk obi
To take for their bridal trousseau
Day after day, Mat-chan had been weaving
Gold-threaded peonies, peacocks, and other treasures
But when told to take any she liked
The plainest turtle-shell pattern is what she chose
I can wear it the longest, she said

Mat-chan looked better than all the others
With her attractive, richly colored nylon scarf
When she lowered her head
And left with the obi
She dove into waters from a shore far more difficult
Than her coming-of-age would ever be
Where are you going?
No one ever dared to ask

They peeled off
Cutouts on the wall
Souvenir pennants from group excursions
Leaving just scotch tape, wistfully waiting
Brush your bangs against it
One hair gets caught
Snuggles up and dangles close

I didn't tell anyone
About her scooping up goldfish
About Machiko or Matsuko or whatever her name was
I didn't tell anyone
About the hot, flushed bodies and furrowed brows
Of the factory girls who had removed their make-up
I didn't tell anyone
About the water of our borrowed bath
About how her fist broke the water's surface
Sending waves, rolling across,
Splash, splash—Sopping, soaking wet
I didn't tell anyone
About the fishy-smelling water droplets
And the fluttering tail of the bright red fish
I didn't tell, I didn't tell
Anyone at all
Did she take what she didn't want to show a soul
And dissolve it in the warm water?
What was it
That dissolved?

She smells of hairspray
Mat-chan, the discolored goldfish

Slips through narrow channels between
Floating photographs, ink oozing out
Between cut-out men and women
Flapping back and forth, back and forth
Flapping back and forth, back and forth
Swimming with her nylon scarf
Where on earth
Could she have
Possibly flowed?

Or was she simply carried away
Down the muddy river flowing by the factory?

JA

THE HEALDS

Clatter clatter—The looms and women fade into dusk
Here I am, still in the thread storeroom
Leaning on the spools of thread, the stiffness in my neck disappeared
A tang of sulphur, the night air the silk spits out
Is a magic lantern
Alone, a single bulb glows
Peering through the hole in the wooden door, the factory
Is a magic lantern

Cold fingers
To touch the healds of the loom
Just at night, when the looms are at rest, he appears, the man
The warp threader
To push the thread through
Into the healds, glittering in a draft of dry wind
Under the bulb's filament
Into their tiny, tiny eyes
Forbidden to blink
Vacant eyes
Because the looms
Before they are hands
Are numberless, nameless eyes
The kind of eyes
That watch every single threaded intersection
So the hanging healds are like the artificial eyes of the factory girls
The night man
Would push it through
First one, then the next
Lightly moistening each one with his tongue
It hurts
The man's back too trembles hard
Grimacing, the healds
Look away
Through the window grating towards the new moon

Are the looms
Marionettes perhaps? At this textile factory

If they don't let it in, they can't work
If they let it in, they get moving eyes, the healds
With a clack
Fold their necks
Towards the man
Releasing pale breath, along the needle
A spreading blur
This ruby-red blood gives them sight

Hung up, one beside the other
From the ceiling,
The sneaking whirlwinds catch
This thread
Then that
All entangled
Arms lift—*banzai!*—legs kicking
Leaning forwards, embracing shoulders, holding bellies, laughing jaws
The man
Races over, desperate to untangle them
Each demanding more attention
More, more, penetrate me
Make me come!
Slyly exposing their breasts
The feminine wiles   of the marionette factory girls
When their coaxing gaze
Returns to the moon
Sweat drips from the man's temples
Running down both cheeks

Right about now
The real flesh and blood bodies of the factory girls
Take their baths at home, boarding houses, and public baths
            Or watch the sleeping faces of their daughters or move to hang up
                                    their phones
No
No
Combing their locks
Their rich hair, tangles in the wind
At precisely eleven o'clock

Forcing it through their hair, the comb
Is reflected in the mirror

Leaning forwards, embracing shoulders, holding bellies, laughing jaws
The marionettes are tangled in threads
The healds are
No, we are
Being manipulated, allowing ourselves to be manipulated, manipulating him
        to manipulate us
As the man rolls up the warp beam
All are pulled up
The roots of our hair, each and every hair follicle
How good it feels!
Delicately
First one strand, then the next, weave together
Hoisting them up, the man works on
The multicoloured threads, our hair,
How alluring we look!

The night factory, the night factory girls, the night coiffeur
All of them, a magic lantern
The single light bulb
Like a pendulum
Swinging
Suddenly
Vanishes
With the warp threader
Before the echoes of the milkman's motor bike

The morning light
Makes the marionettes
Look like looms
But you know
All about the wooden comb the man leaves behind

If you're a factory girl, that is

                                                            CH & RK

GREEN WINGS

So damn itchy
Sprouting
Along the ridge of my back
Wings growing
My cast-off shell falls away so quick and clean
My goodness!
Now I've got these thin arms too?
As I look down, I see the abyss that held me
Was only a small hole, four inches long

No
Before becoming a cicada, I was a little pinky finger
Belonging to Kiyoko, the weaving girl
Seven years, seventy-seven days ago
She was working too carelessly
When she caught my base in the beater
All around me, the dye spread
The chrysanthemum-patterned silk
Grew red as if reflecting the setting sun
Spoiling
The entire roll

After spurting so much blood
She threw me away
Kiyoko
Threw me away
A little part of me was still stuck on
But she twisted and tossed me away
In the backwoods
No
She couldn't stand the fuss
All the other factory girls made
And dashed outside, but later
She returned to look for me, over and over again

Ants swarmed
Fallen leaves covered me

But even after nothing but bones were left
There was something
That wouldn't go away
A flame
Of desire
I remembered with such longing
Such longing
The yolks of the eggs Kiyoko had licked
No spit
I just swallowed
Gulping
Gulping
The sound reverberating
In the dirt

Desire
Reverberates
Twisting
Turning
Forming a pounding pulse

I remembered with such longing
The yolks of the eggs Kiyoko ate
The brown of Kiyoko's eyes
I swallowed down
My own marrow
        From the finger bones
Gulping
Until completely clear

And I transformed
Into a white
Chrysalis

And I grew
And I grew
Even though I'd never flown before
I extended my pale green wings
And swung down and out
To the edge of night

Now I think of urinating
Onto Kiyoko's head
Seven years, seventy-seven days of
Gulping
Gulping
Dripping down
So that she might smell me above

JA

MASAE

Little Masae-chan was a girl, a little girl, an only granddaughter, beloved by her Grandpa.

The man sings on his way to the barn out back to get some charcoal for the hibachi. In his hand, a bucket for charcoal. His silk kimono is chestnut brown with a pine-needle pattern, and the obi around his waist is tied to look like a shellfish with its body peeking out. His clothes might be rather old, but still he's trying his best to look sharp—funny, considering how early in the morning it is. Yasaburō, who had greeted the New Year sixty-three times over the course of his life, is retired from the weaving business, and his son who was set to take over had been taken to the South Seas, leaving behind Masae, his only child, before deployment.

Oh, precious child, oh, precious child! he sings.

It's not just because of his age that steel grey stagnates in the rising tune. The girl is turning three, and her mouth is heavy and still. To put it bluntly, she is mute. It's the old man's masochism that makes him carry his granddaughter's voice in his heart, as he raises his voice so loudly in the mornings.

It's a little premature to use a hibachi halfway through September. Has Masae developed a fever? Most of the worrying people do over snotty, running noses is the result of old folks giving them too much attention. As a maid, it's embarrassing for her to see her retired, old master dirtying his hands with charcoal. He insists, "No worries, I'll take care of it myself."

No.

No one's ever seen her.

No ones's ever seen Masae.

The maid doesn't do much more than place the food trays at the entrance of the small house off to the side of the retired man's property. When the trays come back, the only thing she's ever touched with her chopsticks was the sashimi. "That stubborn old man, he must be getting her to open her mouth wide—*aaaaaah*—and feeding her himself. He's spoiling her, all gentle and soft-like." Knowingly, she tells herself this tall tale as she pulls the bucket up from the well—No, no, she knows what's really going on.

The sliding lattice doors are designed so that the upper and lower parts would slide apart, allowing one to gaze at the moon from inside. As she passes before them, a faint sound—*shariiin, shariiiiiiiiiiiin*. It's a strange sound... Maybe the little girl's a monster made of just skin and bone. There's no way two slices of sashimi per day would be enough for anyone. She utters the spell she uses when frightened. *Kuwabara, kuwabara. Lord, help us.*

He wasn't the sort of fellow who'd deprive a child of dinner as punishment. The old man liked to dote, so much so that he built fires for her with his own hands. The little girl's got to be sensitive to the cold or something. No, she stays in the tokonoma alcove—the part of the house where you'd ordinarily find a flower vase or hanging scroll, not a little girl. Yasaburō felt he needed to do whatever he could to keep her warm, even if it didn't amount to much. After all, she'd been born way down south.

Go ahead. Come right up, slide the doors open. Quietly, gently. You'll see a decorative ebony pillar inside next to the alcove. Right there, next to that. You'll find a large, white-glazed earthenware jar sitting on a red, silk pillow. Now, take a look inside. That's where she is. Right there. In the jar. It's ok, no need to worry. You'll be fine for a moment—it'll take a little while before the old man gets the charcoal to burn.

The sound reverberates across the base of the darkness. *Shariiin, shariiin.* Are your eyes adjusted yet?

She's seated inside...

That's where you'll find Masae.

Step right up and take a look. You'll see she's got three arms on her right side. Three on the left too. Has she got scabies? She's all swollen up like she's infected or something, and she's covered in scabs. She's got two eyes, and each time they flash white, tears roll down, but even so, her eyes seem filled with rage. Yes, she's determined to live.

Ladies and gentlemen, don't avert your eyes. Yes, she's completely mute. She can't speak to herself, much less cry out. Look! She's noticed you; she's curling up even more tightly, with only her eyes turning to peek up at you. Come on, smile at her. After all, she's just a baby, three years old.

Who knows what karma has brought her this fate? Four long whiskers grow from her nose, looking like raw, twisted thread. They're like the thread left behind by the breath of a silkworm; they feel around, all alone, for something in the darkness. *Shariiin, shariiin*—the noise is the sound of her pushing with one hand against the side of the jar as she tries desperately to stand. Each time, she loses her strength, and her nails scrape against the glassy glaze, creating this sound. Goodness, it sounds like a horrifying, weird version of a suikinkutsu.

Uh-oh, there's the sound of the old man's wooden clogs. Quickly, slide the door closed, and come this way.

The tray Yasaburō has brought full of food has feet shaped like those of a cat. He places the burning charcoal in the hibachi with metal chopsticks, then exchanges them for regular chopsticks—well, maybe not entirely regular ones. More elegant than usual. Short, children's chopsticks stained yellow and covered with transparent lacquer. In the thin tips of the chopsticks that drip from his wrinkled fingers is a freshly sliced piece of sashimi, a translucent piece of sea bream, white touched with pale red. *Masae-chan, breakfast time,* he says in a strangely, sweet voice. The old man's flirtatious tone reverberating over the sound *shariin, shariin* seems weirdly out of place.

And her way of munching down food is also something to behold. Yasaburō tries hard, over and over, to get her to open her mouth—*aaaaaah, aaaaaah*—and put in the sashimi. She curls up tightly and keeps her mouth firmly shut. Not having much choice, he holds it right in front of her eyes, and after a few moments, she begins to squirm. The three limbs on her left side hold the sea bream firmly down. *This is mine,* her eyes glare. Then her right hands also begin to squirm around, making the same movements over and over. But take a good look! The first and thickest hand on both her left and right have ridiculously long pointers and middle fingers. With the fingernails of the first hand on her right, she touches the red-tinged piece of fish, and acts as if she's about to pick it up and toss it in her mouth.

However, her other thin arms appear, like the tongues of a gecko. Two white arms poke out from both sides of her neck, so slender they look like they might break. Then quietly, the palms of these new hands curl up like she's scooping water from a spring, and she cups the reddish flesh she's just grabbed in her fingernails. Carefully, carefully, as if holding a sacred offering in a white bowl. Her mouth distorts forlornly, her left eye quivers, and quietly, carefully, she partakes. With her sweet, little tongue. Surely Yasaburō can't be the only one to feel his heartstrings tighten at her mealtime modesty, so out of sorts with her ugly appearance.

She doesn't even finish half the slice of sashimi. She makes the first hints of a smile at her grandpa, perhaps wanting to thank him for the food, then folds her right hands and lays them down flat. Shaking her whiskers, she withdraws. Into the shell of herself. With the great shears on her left, she closes off the entrance.

All the remains on the floor of the darkness is a beautiful turban shell.

Those of you readers who are especially perceptive have probably already figured out the mystery. Masae is a hermit crab.

The old man's son Masao, stationed in a regiment in Kagoshima, was a funny fellow and sent various types of southern shells to his father, hoping he might work them into the designs for his obi. Shells are an auspicious pattern for young women to wear. Since his retirement, Yasaburō didn't have any desire to create new patterns, so he gave the shells as calcium fertilizer to his bonsai. Before long, Masao would be sent to the island of Luzon. His bones would never return.

That day,
Oh, my goodness!
One of them crawled up—one of the shells. Just imagine! Creeping, crawling, across the wood grains of the veranda boards.
"Masao."
Yasaburō dropped his pipe. At that moment, the pine needles in the pattern of his kimono all floated up, stood straight, and burst into bluish flame. The countless thorns of flame wandered about, blowing wildly as if pointing toward the ceiling, then they shot through openings in the wood panel above the door.
The smoke stroked his father's trembling back. For a moment, its vague moments even seemed to wave a hand at him. Could it merely have been the spirit-flame of the silkworms?

Hermit crabs don't come from around here, other than when people sell them at stalls during festivals. What does that mean? Do hermit crabs abandoned by their owners, children who consume things like hungry ghosts, change their shells for the empty ones at the bottom of bonsai plants?
Perhaps the reason he gave her the name Masae,
And not Masao
Comes less from his desire for descendants, but from his sense of humor
Crawling onto the seashore to stem the tide of tears.

JA

FLARED SKIRT

It was...

I was…

It was the spring holidays just before I started girls' high. Our tabby cat Buchi had kittens, well, just one really. But then she was very old. She twisted it out with all her strength, wearing herself out. Furious like the edge of a knife, *eeeek-mew eeeek-mew,* the tiny mouse-like creature snuggled tight against her breast, as Buchi tried desperately to hide the little one from view. Like an unwed mother birthing a bastard child.

A while back, that first bleeding happened to me too. On the narrow back deck where we paid the newspaper boy in the evenings, suddenly, my flared skirt was stained. The next day, mother cooked up twenty cups of celebratory red bean rice.

"Miss, now you're finally one of us—a woman," said Kat-chan, one of the weaving girls, pulling up the skirt on the clothesline to expose the inside.

"They're the latest fashion," said Misa-chan, giving me some peach-colored panties.

And Shimo-yan, who fixed the looms, stroked my bottom with his work-gloved hands. "So round, so plump."

It's wasn't a story for the papers! It was my period!

Mummm!

Buchi was originally a stray. But back then, there were no purebred house cats. Scrounging for food scraps under the eaves, slyly crawling in under the kotatsu, she was shameless. When I tried to stroke her back, she slipped past me with a hiss. She snorted and turned away. I never managed to get my arms round her.

It was hard, wasn't it? It was for me. When Shimo-yan, with his tobacco stink, stroked my bottom, blood oozed out, so slimy. And then I had to go out into town wearing the same panties as Misa-chan. And then during the three o'clock break, when the front teeth of the factory workers lined up for the red bean rice, my inner void clenched emptily. They were saying somebody had buried a mouse in Kat-chan's lower belly. Six months already.

It was the night when we took down the New Year pine decorations.

Huh? An abandoned child?

It must have been a factory girl again.

The crying was so heart-wrenching, coming from the factory yard. I pulled on my hanten to look near the base of the fence, and there she was. Buchi. Yowling with a cry that would melt frost, rubbing her belly along the ground.

Waaah—meioooowww!

As the tomcat started to ride her, the cougar forced up her tail and stuck her bottom out. After the deed was done—*raaww*—her unyielding willfulness returned and she drove him off, that male cat from next door.

Daughter and heir, only child. Just like me.

I'll finish at the Girl's High School, get a husband, inherit the factory, continue to pay Kat-chan and Misa-chan, their children, and even their mothers-in-law. My marital intercourse will feed them.

It's my monthly flow—my moon drops

That feed them!

The factory house mice

All of you—congratulations!

Rising up

In me

The blood red new moon

Quivering like a trembling heart

Shining

Dripping

A sticky……. trail of drops

This is it—genuine red rice!

Look at it!

Shimo-yan! Don't slip and drown

Hey, Kat-chan. Tasty, eh?

Newspaper man! Come on, go ahead!

Take as many photos as you like!

My smiling, my shamelessness—inside my flared skirt

Don't stand on ceremony! Go for it!

The next morning, when Mum opened the shutters—there was a stain. On the tatami before the altar to the family dead. There was Buchi. She looked up at us with dark, shadowed eyes, her mouth thick with filthy wetness.

She'd eaten it. Her own sweet, lovely little house mouse. Impaled on her canines.

          I don't want to be
                    A woman
          I want to go back
          As the mouse
                    In Mum's belly, me too
          Hey, Buchi
          Couldn't you squeeze anything out
          Of those bony breasts?
          No one fed you, did they? No white rice?

     With only a sidelong glance, the cat soon left the factory, ignoring me as I wept.

CH & RK

BACKYARD

A citrus tree stands there
Half rotten, half sprouting new stems
Like a tongue clinging to light
It rattles dryly
A lizard with lovely bluish-purple stripes
Dashes across fallen leaves
And stops abruptly
The buds of the angelica tree
With curled tails
Quickly grow fluff into thorns and bend back leaves
At some point grandmother appears beside me
"Watch out! If it stings you
It'll hurt for ten whole days"

I gaze at the ants transporting their food
Wondering if they are invisible foam bubbling from the earth
Dislocated and crawling, dislocated and crawling
Looking down on them
They toil so busily
Wriggling like a transparent creature
A wet, earthy aroma fills the air
From the corner of the yard
The butterbur stretching its neck among the ferns
Has probably let out a sigh
The lizard scurries across the threshold of the cleaned-out storeroom

The rocks are warm
The thin weight of sleepiness crawls up the back of my neck
Everything grows light before my eyes
"Give the plants some water"
Stretching toward me is a high-pitched voice
That curves gently to the left like a bent bow
I run across the backyard

I run
Across the backyard where
The chrysanthemums were planted

The bulges of grandmother's fingers
Had hollowed out the dirt around the roots
"It will grow bigger"
I had watered it and
The leaves had fluttered
Beside Inari, the fox god's shrine
A little bird bends in the air
As if its feet were being tickled
It chases
It has intercourse
The tone of its warbling is as if
It is raining though the sun is out
From the shade of the large locust tree
A child looks this way through her narrow eyes

Dig in the dirt
I just wanted to dig in the dirt
Perhaps I was just being dull, perhaps strong and steady
A citrus tree stands there
Half rotten, half sprouting new stems
Like a tongue that clings to light
Before long
The heavy machinery will come
Before we see summer
This lot will be vacant

Dig in the dirt
I just wanted to dig in the dirt
My right shoulder throbs
A white moth flits by
And the skin inside
My muddy boots
Suddenly goes cold

JA

COLORED GLASS

I'll raise it in my tummy
I'll break it
Squashing the bitter worm in my teeth
If I swallow it down
I doubt I'll spit out a moth
Or that it'll fly out as a butterfly
I suppose it'll stay a silkworm spitting out silk forever — *factory and
no upward
mobility*

          Maybe it'll become a spinning wheel turning its own neck
        The axle letting out a rhythmic rattle under the sawtooth roof
     Its arm extended as it turns itself
   Its knees shaking ever so slightly

I'll swallow it down
The silkworm
Down the well of my throat
Where it rebounds in the pit of my stomach
This little worm will spit out a lifeline
And crawl from the watery depths
Forgetting its dreams of flying through the air

          In this strange factory, the worm spins
        In the spinning wheel
          The raw silk thread winding around before our eyes
       The scissors slip in, and it is bound up tightly
    Pulse throbbing from the effort

Warawara   *Are you inviting the thread?*
     Carried away
Somosomo   *Are you touching the thread?*
     Laughed at
Sawasawa   *Are you lining up the thread?*
     Slandered
Moshimoshi   *Are you resentful of the thread?*
     Forgotten
     Extolled
     Untold

Sing: *Roll your hands   round and round   pull your eyes flat*
           Roll your hands   round and round   pull your eyes flat
           Roll your hands   round and round   pull your eyes out

I swallowed it!
The eternal silkworm
On its mission forever
Crawling through the labyrinth of my bowels
The bitter worm squashed in my teeth
In the rustling thread it spins
It ties itself up
Withdraws
And sleeps

It cannot sleep,
I cannot sleep
Sing: *Roll your hands   round and round   pull your eyes flat*
           Roll your hands   round and round   pulled my eyes out
I hold it over my head

                    There is a factory floating like an isle inside
                        Its head turns round and round
                    While blind silkworms glow
                Under the colored glass window

                                                            JA

CLUSTERS OF FALLING STARS

Just how many millions of e-mails
Could have been deleted?

*

The dye factory Asako's father owned was put up for auction
Two months after the change in leadership
At the branch office of the bank
The rules of the free market had crushed
Local factories strangled by loans
But she was fourteen when she learned
Speculators had determined
In which order the ax would fall

The golden boy of the day, tech CEO Horie Takafumi, was arrested
Nine months after they hired the new section chief
At the Special Investigations Unit of the Tokyo Prosecutor's Office
The rules of the Security Exchange Law had governed
The price fixing of company stocks
But Asako thought speculators determined
In which order the ax would fall

"You can sweat but still not get ahead," her father had said
"You can buy people's hearts with money," Horie had said
"I want to expose wrongdoing that'll enrage all you who sweat for a living,"
             the section chief had said
                                  Even after the big arrest,
                         Did they investigate
                    The companies swollen
              From buying up other corporations
        With the speed the investigation deserved?

She heard that well over a hundred computers and cell phones were
        collected
She heard that was because all the important transactions were done over
        e-mail
She heard that two hours before the police came in it was leaked to the news

She heard that the investigators had fretted that most of the evidence
                    was gone
She heard that some of it had already been wiped away

Just how many millions of e-mails
Could have been deleted?
Asako thinks to herself
Perhaps an astronomical number
They must have hit delete countless times
So the e-mails would never be found again
It must have been quite the busy week
For the company which fortunately avoided
Being number one on the speculators' block

                    *

What do you wish for
When wishing upon a shower
Of falling electric stars?
She heard Horie once wrote
"Number One in the World"
As his wish on a card at the Star Festival
If you look up tonight
Once again
—Right there!
Another huge cluster of falling stars

                                                            JA

SHADOWS

In this place suddenly thrown into disarray
It is impossible to distinguish
Between what is garbage
What is not and what is still useable
So much earth, sand and dust
Has fallen that
Everywhere I see
A great can of refuse
The mucus I wipe on my sleeve is black
My throat and lungs are eroded
Let it be, just the way it is…
Listless and resigned, I roll up my sleeves
And muster what little enthusiasm I can

I can't let this be turned into a vacant lot
At least until I pick up the marble
I dropped here before things got this way
At least until I pick through the refuse
And save at least one suitcase's worth of pure junk

This place will be completely stripped away
This place will disappear
I must stretch out my hands
And hold fast to
The shadows of this land
Even if only in a suitcase I will surely
Never open again

JA

INTO THE WORLD

GIVE US MORNING

[handwritten: Tsunami + war in Iraq]

Morning's the time we count the dead
In the newspapers, in the hospitals, on the roads, on the seashores
In the rubble that was once our homes
Possess us all the more, Amenouzume-san
The morning is still not enough
We still cannot count them all
We still cannot carry them all
Dance more for us, Amenouzume-san
Put a green twig in your hair
And call to them *[handwritten: dance + performance]*
Give the dead
To morning
Possess them, call to them

> *It's me, the girl floating here this whole time*
> *It's me, Mama's boy crouched down*
> *It's me, the boy with the right arm wrenched off*
> *I want to see you again, I want to see you again*
> *A bullet to the temple*
> *I scratch my throat, it hurts*
> *Now I'm sinking as far as I can go*
> *Why? Why was I the boy*
> *Blown aside by the bomb blast?*
> *The fingers of flame came in no time*
> *I struggle but there's only sand, I struggle but there's only sand*
> *One lung was crushed by the ceiling*
> *Left alone like this, where will I float?*
> *I wait for an extended hand*
> *Here I am, here I am*
> *I want to escape this blood-bathed school*
> *With my girlish eyes still open wide*
> *I know this is my last breath*
> *I am fed up with the roar of the bombs*
> *The sea has raised its clenched fist*

Morning's the time we count the dead
On the TV news, in the embassies, in the community centers

In the rubble that was once our buildings and our mosques
Possess us all the more, Amenouzume-san
The morning is still not enough
The morning is still not enough
The morning is still not enough
Dance for us all the more, Amenouzume-san
Claw the milk from your breast, shake your hair wildly
Pound your feet on the ground
And dance
Spin your arms round, shake off your sweat
Bend back your neck
And dance, dance
More
More
Sway your spine, lift your legs
Shake your hips
More
More
Set your womanly shadow on fire
Open your womanly shadow
And call for them
And dance for them
And possess them
And gather
The dead
To the shadow

Give them to morning
Give us morning
The time we count the corpses

JA

COME, COME, FALL FAST ASLEEP

It was a mystery, praying
Became our daily ritual, in the morning
Newspapers,
A male member, slushy, sloshing,
Trying to hold back, presses hard into a grand pot,
Wet with a woman's arousal, and stirs
No
I'm not talking
About the erotic stories in some men's paper
Ever since that day, wasn't that the icon
That adorned the front pages of our news?

It was a monster,
A fiery pillar of lust, the fuel rod
In the uterus of the nuclear reactor
It had lost control, a real stud
Slushy, sloshing, stewing, brooding
Melting and dripping out, whoa!

We had pretty much forgotten
The electric brains of our computers
Had eaten into our brains
That thing down there

Still the nuclear plant keeps doing it
In the mere half-life of an infant
Bunches more electric children are born with a wail
While we sing the lullaby
Come, come, fall fast asleep

JA

GALAPAGOS

Just gossip! The damn economy is
Nothing but a fairy tale! Stock prices,
Come on and just do it!
        Make fun of them all the more
I'm sick of it
All this goth clothing, all this Uniqlo-ing

It's a mess! Eros
Left out all the time! Thanatos
Bring it back to life!
        Alienate them all the more
Those incessant cellphones
Those Microsoft monsters

        ——————— *Isn't that all you'd ever let us wear?*
        Wasn't that our national uniform?
        Before the quake
        The tsunami of the recession
        All we ever worried about?

It
Is our protective wear
It thrives on adversity
It can withstand high waves
Up to six meters tall
No
It's more like swimming gear
It looks like it might drown
In the cold global
Womb of grotesque globalism
In Lehman Brothers
Salarymen
Don't want anything
Don't say anything
Won't do anything, won't do it anymore
Girls, boys, the intermediate sex
No more procreating, unisex

Just look
At that fission
They say they can't get any fusion
Between those sperm-like neutrons

Things have just been let go! Nuclear fission
Just exposed! The womb of the reactor dome too
Fuel rods *(nenryōbō)*, safety hats *(anzenbō)*, egg cells (ransaibō), stinginess
         (kechinbō), thieves *(dorobō)*,
Refrigerators *(reibō)*, heaters *(danbō)*,
Babies *(akanbō)*, deceased *(hotokenbō)*, floating *(ukabō)* on the great plain of
         the sea, on the verge of screaming *(orabō)*,
The reactor building about to fly off *(buttobō)*,
Embankments *(teibō)*, conspiracies *(inbō)*, ministerial offices *(kanbō)*,
                  Unbelievabō
                  Incredibō
TEPCO
                  Puts on their Uniqlo
         To bulwark against
The tsunami

                  No nuclear dome?
         Then we'll make electricity
      In our con-domes
Is a half-life
Good enough

For us?

                                                      JA

HALF A PAIR OF SHOES

The red poppy is in bloom
A leather shoe, just half a pair,
Lies washed up on the seashore
Laces still tied

As the poppy bends
And drops dew from its petals
The shoe sighs faintly
The flower shakes itself off
And the dirty shoe
Starts to open
Its eye

Mostly likely
No landscapes are reflected
In that eye, deep as an old well,
Memories
Soak through
The poppy can only caress
She extends her leaves
Toward the chest-like instep

        —— *You cannot break me, the waves*
            Cannot wash away
            My worn-down heel
            And my folds

               They draw near
          The gaze of the shoeless boy
      Going as far as the water's edge
If the poppy gazed in
How clear that eye would be
A fire, like a small fish's fin
At the bottom of an old well

        —— *The sea cannot extinguish*
            The frank, pale flame

At the depths of my existence
For the sea too is an enormous eye

What light must the wave have emitted
In that moment
As it watered and rushed
Surging in anger
Far from shore
As the other shoe was swallowed

———— *Did the school of sardines*
See the circle
Of blue flame
Drawn in my eyes?

The poppy is trembling again
No
It is the wind
The flower stands naked
Dropping its petals
Into the well

It is an umbilical cord
The tip of the shoelace
Falling into the depths of the eye
Where the boy tries to grab on

Down it crawls

JA

JA

JA

LOTS AND LOTS

Tsutomu and Isamu—
Those names were popular among boys back then
But we weren't even paying attention when
One of Osamu's creations, our number one author,
Crossed the sea and changed
His name to Astro
Hmmmm... Think about it
          To tell the truth
It didn't even come across as some cruel joke
When Atom
The boy hero came calling
From the islands where the atomic bombs once fell

When did we realize
What his name really meant?
Hmmmm... Think about it
I wanted to be friends with Uran
This is no cruel joke
All of us kids were that way back then
Each one of us with an atomic reactor in our hearts
Maybe we were the ones who changed his name
Calling him
Atom

When we called him that
We cut off
The root
Of the word
For the future, for the universe
For our own peaceful uses, as a nation that had suffered through the bomb
I don't want to blame
The young Tezuka
The adults wanting to sell dreams
The children wanting to lose themselves in dreams
Went right along too
With his inklings and the iron-arms
Like filings to a magnet

Lots of them

And lots of them
He would not have been able to draw him
If that were really his name
He could not depict him as *Genko*, a girl robot
That was what we needed
      Right then
A new nuance
For the future, for the universe
For our twisted peace
The name Atom
Split off from the atom
And the atomic bomb

      ————The reason his power source
      Was swept out to sea that day
      Was because it wasn't part of him
      It had been cut off from the start
           The language on these islands
      Gets rid of roots, cuts them off with katakana
      Long before the earthquake
          If so, then

It was okay to use that name
          So that's why
      His name, all sparkling clean
Was used
Lots
And lots
Until smeared with filth and mud

What we have are not fifty-four reactors
We have fifty-four Atoms standing there at the water's edge
Of the four that the waves swallowed
Three blew themselves up, one's innards failed
The jets in their legs
Rained down iodine, cesium, strontium
His little brother Cobalt chased after him
Through fields, mountains, towns

Among people, livestock, butterflies
The furnaces in the three Atoms' hearts
Melted down and collapsed
                    Making
His little sister Uran seethe, the fission wouldn't stop
Professor Ochanomizu and Dr. Tenma were killed
Into the sea poured
An accumulation of tears
From his kind heart
Some of the other Atoms
Also stood atop fault lines
Some grew old, their metallic exhaustion began
And then
Even though we shut them down
We still couldn't find a place to get rid of them
This is our one and only world
Not a manga in which we can blow things up in space
                    There he was
Mulling over the laws of robotics
"I was born to make people happy"
Perhaps all this hurt him more than humanity

                    *

At the edge of the water
Fifty-four severed heads
Four of them
Eyes lowered, noses lowered, piling penance upon penance day after day
One dropping countless chemical children on a land of withered trees
One killing countless chemical children in a sea without salt or moon
One surprised as it measures the dead Atom's legs and the living Atom's eyes
On its scale of tangled serpents only to find they weigh the same
One dead and sicker than before
Coughing within its concrete sarcophagus

                    *

A single butterfly crosses the Becquerel Straits.

                    *

A face appears below the ground
The sad face of a sick man
The grass sprouts and sways
Countless hairs begin to tremble
From the sad, sick surface
The sad face of Atom appears
Tears dripping
Dripping tears
   At this moment
Thin roots
Hairy roots
Cilia from root tips
Cilia covered in faint hair

They will grow, won't they?
We will make them grow, won't we?
In the soil that is the language of these islands
In the deep darkness at its base

An object mired in karma
   Will he ever
      Be allowed
To rest in peace?

JA

EH-JANAIKA, EH-JANAIKA

Why does the phrase *Eh-janaika* (It's alright, isn't it?)
Drive people to dance about like crazy, the way it does?
However it's repeated
No one would dance to
Yoi dewa arimasenka (Why, don't you think that it would be just fine?)
Ii-janaika (It's alright, isn't it?) comes close but
The act of pulling your mouth apart to say *Ii*
Seems self-centered and
Doesn't have the force to round up a whole mob of people under the moon
Eh
Through a lightly opened mouth
Functions as a vowel, but
When stretched out, as in *Eeeh-*
Descends the deep well of your throat
Finds the bucket at the bottom and draws it back up
Makes a turnabout with *ja*
And then with *naika*, gets soaked
That is to say
Eh(↗), *ja*(⌢↘), *naika*(↘) ↗ ↘
Forms an eternal cycle of large and small waves

I wonder just where this
Eh-janaika comes from
Ii-janeika in the
Northern Kantō dialect exudes a high-handed angle (↓)
But doesn't quite have the force of a wave
Eh-yanaika in the Kansai dialect
Has a softer crest on its wave(⌢↘)
But still lacks the force that would swallow people in
And if this is the case
Perhaps it's from somewhere central, like Mino or Mikawa
Where words like this might be born, I suspect
It must have spread
Freely throughout Japan
Precisely because it is not a vernacularism
The *ja* is a resonant voiced consonant in which you might hear the
Distant sounds of Tsugaru "jo"ngara music

Where you put the *ja* (snake)-skin across the shamisen
While thinking about the remnants of Japonesia

And so what would happen then if
We translate *Eh-janaika* to English?
"It's alright, isn't it?"
Has a rising intonation (↗)
Along with a tag question sleeping beside it (↘)
And you find that peeking out from behind
Is a sense of "yeah, yeah," someone's calling you
⌁↘

Sō-da, Sō-da (That's right, that's right)
Sō-ka village's
Sonchō-san (Mayor)
Drank some *sō-da* (soda)
And *shinda sō-da* (died, they say)
The *sō-shiki* (funeral) steamed bun
Is *dekkeh sō-da* (pretty big, they say)
⌁↘
This is a joke-song from the Shōwa period
Which makes me imagine a devilish little child
Singing such a song, while sitting atop the shoulders
Of folks in a mob, storming a warehouse

Furthermore
The brilliance of *Eh-janaika* might be that it is
A translation of *Namu Amida Butsu*
Six hundred years in the making
And under that moon, at the head of the group
Ringing the bell
Is the ghost of Ippen-san
We've invoked

And singing with him
Instantly our hips begin to move
It is the age of degeneration

Can we break through it, this "present moment"?

Eh-janaika, Eh-janaika

Eh-janaika, Eh-janaika
Eh-janaika, Eh-janaika
Eh-janaika, Eh-janaika

SUPPLEMENTS

Vitamins A, B, C, D, E, F, G
Lipoic acid and malic acid, picolinic acid and pyruvic acid
Coenzymes and chondroitins, selenium and andrographis
Anthocyanin, alpha-carotene, isoflavone, gingko extract
A whole bowlful of supplements
Instead of the morning meal
Vitamins H, I, J, K, L, M, N
Potassium and calcium, magnesium and germanium
Glucosamine and glycogen, taurine and turmeric
Cat's claw, chitosan, eye drops made of maple, melatonin
A second bowlful of supplements
And still nothing for my skin!
Placenta, pueraria, collagen, squalane
Then there's those menstrual cramps
Progesterone, pasque flower, chasteberry, evening primrose
And if they'll rev me up there's the men's meds
Zinc, selenium, arginine, ginseng and Viagra too!
Hōhokekyo
Hōhokekyo
Kekyo kekyo kekyo kekyo, hohohōhokekyo
I feel like I'm flying
Looking down on the whole world
I feel nauseous
This won't work. Relax. For relaxation try
Carotene and resistin, theanine and valerian
And let me throw in something to prevent senility
I gulp down gingko extract once again
Polyphenol is now out of date but
One can cover the old-fashioned supplements with
Acerola, chlorella, ebios, biofermin

Vitamins O, P, Q, R, S, T, U
Flavonoids and grape seeds, marigolds and oligopeptides
A thirtieth bowlful of supplements
Vitamins V, W and X, Y, Z
A thirty-first bowlful of supplements
And still I can go on

Still there are the things written only in kanji
Luohanguo, lidanyan, licorice, cordyceps
Wheat germ oil, flax oil, egg yolk oil
Lactic acid bacilli, natto bacilli, colon bacilli
Folic acid, nucleic acid, medium-chain fatty acids, monounsaturated fatty acids
Pills to fight crotch itch and athlete's foot, pills to lift a man into seventh heaven,
        pills of potassium cyanide and quince and aconite
Ointment to make a shiny head grow hair in a flash, powder to make a body grow
        ghostly thin, beans for off-the-cuff word play......

I will not get caught
I will not get caught no matter how long it takes
I am a slippery, smooth pill
Sliding slickly down the throat
The supplement is I
α, β, γ, δ
Hiragana, katakana, kanji, romanization
Alliteration at the beginning, rhymes at the end
The words tangle together
The words tangle turning
So rhythmic they bring tears to the eyes
A heavy rhythm within a light-hearted one
Here within this poem

                *

Did it dissolve?
Is the mystery solved?

What you have swallowed is language itself

                                                                    JA

SOUL DANCE

The creature crawled from the midnight mountain of rubble with its long,
        skinny tail
A tail that writhes
It is the bowels of the soul
Glowing fluorescent green
In its half-transparent head, the creature bares its buck teeth
Its eyes have no center though it fixes its gaze
Undulates then leaps
Leaps
I won't eat the flesh of human necks, they're too hard
People are no good at handling things
They just bow over and over like fools
I could soften them with vinegar
A gutter comes apart at the joints and dirty water splashes on the road below
The soul-goblin picks at it with its claws
Before our eyes, it crosses a cable, and on the shoulder of an electrical pole
The soul
Does a shake-dance
Swinging its intestines back and forth
This is how I get hungry again
The world these days is so full of trash, I'm sick of eating it
I don't need your stupid offerings
Stretching, shrinking, it begins to digest, pulsing and green
And eventually
Drops of fire rain from its behind
A tiger cat raises its chin and sends up a yell—*Meow, amigo*
The soul undulates then leaps
It leaps
Leaps up
Skips over stupidly beautiful lashes curled up with an eyelash curler
Drops onto the collarbone of a boy popular and powerless
Hops down a pendulous breast that cannot resist gravity
Gallops across know-it-alls clinging to the nose hairs of authority
Undulates and leaps
Leaps, undulates, and leaps again
Leaps
A beautiful, strange intestinal bird, pulsing green

Baring its buck teeth
The garbage of Disaster-day and
Drunk-day (*hiccup*) both belong to the soul
Hey, shall I pick at
Whatever time remains for you?
Grab at it? Dig into it with my claws?
Damn, it's much too hard, It won't turn, neither will your head
Meow, amigo
The soul taps
Steps, shake-dances
Scatters drop of fire
And rows a bicycle
I want to be hungry again
I'm a living, sexual, sacred body so I'm sensitive where my body stagnates
So then
I'll grab, I'll dig in, I'll do gymnastics
For whatever time remains for you
Hey you!
You haughty good-for-nothing!
That stinky durian you're offering? I won't take it, no way!

JA

MEMBRANE

Long, long ago,
In Ancient Egypt—3000 BC—
They were made, it is said, of billy-goat bladders and piglet appendixes
So they really were membranes
To begin with
Slaves who carried the pyramid stones
Surely in the night
Not only swilled
But slipped it on and humped

Long ago
In Restoration England—seventeenth century—
A king as merry as a piggywig, giddy as a billy goat—Charles—
Pumped thirty-four babes
Into his mistresses' wombs
"Your majesty, pardon me," said the doctor to the king. "Might you, perhaps,
Contain yourself?"
And then he slipped the cow's casing on him
(It was offal—the pigskin—too little—had split)—

Condom was his name
That doctor

The alpha occupier
Adolf, invading Poland's
Factories of seamless rubber
Distributed, I believe
To German soldiers

Vast numbers

(Those made for the Japanese army
Were named *Charge!* and *Iron Helmet*, I've heard
No joke)

What feelings, I wonder,
Came and came
Into the thin rubber bag

Into the swirling pool of hormones and pheromones
Into the skinny crack between pig and humankind
Yes—
The rubbed split between the hole and the pole
Five thousand years ago—
No—
Further back, at the dawn of pants—

Doctor Condom Sir was his name!
That doctor
Was already there, surely
In the shadow of Adam's
Figleaf
Slipping it out of his doctor's bag

"Sir, please, might you contain yourself?"

                    The 0.02 mm membrane
                Swills fluid
        It stinks
It reeks

It must be the only doctor
For all *humankind!*

JC & RK

EXISTENCE

Which one is the girl you want? One monme's worth of flowers
That one is the girl we want. One monme's worth of flowers

Before we knew for sure the girl was even here,
She'd been endowed with life. Long before.
Still in her glass altar, we defrost her in the microwave—the kiss to seal the oath. Wasn't the matchmaker who smelled of disinfectant in fact a white-robed angel?

When one has eyes to see small, small, small things, existence also becomes so small, small, small. You were almost six feet tall, you say? The same size as an old-time yardstick. Now you're only sixty microns. Please write in big block letters, write in permanent ink—you must have heard this wish countless times when names were written on the sperm collection cup. Even a white-robed angel can't see the faces of little tadpoles without putting on her reading glasses. Will things turn out all right or not?—Fate is fifty-fifty. This or that? Fifty-fifty. Really interesting. Even in our information society, what happens right next to us is still a question of symbols.

When one has eyes to see small, small, small things, existence also becomes so big, big, big. Am I really me? The idea we each have a mind that exists beyond matter is probably just a fantasy cooked up by Christians. In this cup, there are two hundred million of me. Me, me, me! In material terms, there's more of me than the entire population of the great Japanese archipelago. I could make my own Great Empire of Japan all by myself! I could cause a revolution at any moment! The possibilities are enormous! All I'd have to do is tap these sleeping kids and wake them up. Break the freezer lid, turn the battleship march as loud as it'll go, and the tadpoles will start springing out one after the next—jumping, jumping, jumping, jumping. Like hitting it big in pachinko. Congratulations! I swim four millimeters per minute, that's how the angel appraised me—I'll be a real lady killer, knocking up the widows!

We're glad she lost, one monme's worth of flowers
We're glad we mock, one monme's worth of flowers

Let's try again: Paper-scissors-rock.
Me, me, me, they say, one in two hundred million
Not him, not him, not him, they say, one in three hundred million

The midwife hears, Is it here yet? Here yet? Here yet?
The sperm bet their lives on the order determined by the game

In the dish, eyes still can't see
Let's try again: Paper-scissors-rock
This is life in the dish
At least until they float belly up

Don't you know, the world of your existence
Is the world of our afterlife?

JA

OF GODS AND SMALL ANIMALS

MOHEI'S FIRE

As soon as I got out of the station, I was in front of a high-rise building under construction, two construction cranes lifting their long necks into the air. I walked down the left side of an excavated path through a town on the edge of old downtown Tokyo, with a bridge at my side where a carillon rings on the hour. I walked past shops selling jellied sweet potato cake and deli foods, and I pressed the elevator button to an apartment with a teahouse on the ground floor. The door was dark green, far in the back. Takejirō-san welcomed me with his sturdy bare feet, bowing many times.

While his left hand kept scratching his neck, under his clean-cut hair, his short gray eyelashes seemed to brush against each other as he recalled this and that, telling me stories. Eighty-some years ago, when he was born, this place was a farming village. They grew leeks, ginger and mustard spinach, put their baskets on a cart and took them to the market in Komagome, called "Yachaba." And although it is now sunken into a culvert, the Yata River, a clear stream about four yards wide, once ran in front of the Inari shrine. They would clean the soil off of the harvested vegetables in the washing area under the big nettle tree and catch small fish in a net. There were even days when a giant carp would swim upstream from the Shinobazu-no-ike pond, through the Yata river flowing into it. There were no excavations in those days, and a slope of about nine feet would just continue on through the woods...

His hoarse voice broke between every single word, making me think of a slightly rusty scythe as it cropped bundles of stem fiber. I listened to him while straining the backs of my eyelids, trying to focus on a very distant scenery that was now long gone. At that moment, Takejirō-san burst into a small laugh, and hesitantly said, "This is a bit funny... A strange thing...," while a faint rose-color filled in his wrinkled cheeks. I caught his infectious laugh, as he began the following story.

*

Grandpa Mohei has long since left us, but this was back when he was young, and the young folks around here used to gather in the morning and go over to Senjū to work.

One day while it was still very, very dark, our grandpa called upon his friends and went to work. They followed the empty field path, rubbing their sleepy eyes and yawning.

They had just about reached Nippori when, for some reason, a single long candle sprouted in their way, towering over him. It must have been the work of a fox or a tanuki. The candle was clutched by a tail, which was also on fire. So Mohei bent over and peered down but could not see what was going on. He tried scaring it by smacking the ground with a piece of wood, like a cane, but the candle stayed there without moving an inch. The red flame was blocking his way, adamantly not letting him pass.

What to do…?

Mohei then flipped around so his rear end faced forward. He tapped his cane while walking backwards. And at that, the old fox flipped up his tail in surprise and took to his heels and disappeared.

*

…So the story went.

A while later, Grandpa tended some plants and is said to have made a very beautiful weeping plum tree, called the "Weeping Mohei." But one day he lost all of his property because of a large fire some stranger had set. All the houses down the block also burned down. From then on, he even came to fear electricity, let alone the thatching on the roof. Could it be that the electric currents that ran through the wires appeared to him like arrows of fire? Those were dark, black nights. They say that no matter how hard the people around him tried to convince him to do otherwise, he would not hear a word of it. The whole family just went on guarding the precious and very thin light of the paper lantern until Mohei-san passed away. It was the early Shōwa period.

As I listened slowly to his story, the paper lantern sitting upon the thin plate gradually began to overlap with the candle held by the fox. Wavering, the two flames become one. Was this the lovely light that twinkled at the bottommost depth of Mohei-san's heart after that seething fire? He entered the darkness every night, carrying with him a small flame that grew sweeter the more it burned. The foxes bent their bodies and came running in one by one. The smell of the burning hair on their soft tails moved to the left and to the right, with strangely wavering clusters of fire streaming behind.

This light has remained lit, faintly but firmly, at the bottom of Takejirō-san's memory. His wife, who was hanging around the door at first, joined the conversation partway and sat next to him, saying that she had never heard such a story in the sixty or so years they had been together. Takejirō-san said he had finally, with his own mouth, shared the story he had heard as a child from his grandmother as she put him to bed. Hearing this unexpected story while seated before the old couple, I felt as if I had been given a small portion of that spark of fire from the palm of their hands.

If you dig in the ground around here, you still come across old foxholes. They contain a deep, distant air, like the inside of a vase. Beneath the ground, under the office buildings and homes, phantom foxes lurk, running around to protect that light. And just what kind of voice do they wrap around it?

Like being excited or dazed... I remember quickly passing the shadows of the cranes by the station, but returning home, I find today's train ticket in my pocket and wonder if I flew past the ticket gate too...

YN & SN

THE TANIGUKU

The surface of water splits
Carrying algae from the deep
And on its breath
The taniguku

Dancing dizziness
One eye is black
One eye is blue
The taniguku
While dancing
Whirls
The whirling eye of morning
Puffing out the warts
On its back
From both its upper
And lower mouths
Gaping
Water bubbles forth and
Whirls

The eastern clouds
Look in and
Shine seductively
The taniguku
Dances and
Whirls
The whirling eye of morning
Its webbing
Out of sight
Both its upper
And lower mouths
Gape and smile
Showing a row of teeth
Whirling

Whirling

Carrying algae
The taniguku
The taniguku
Calling
Morning into it
Together they stick out
Their tongues
A water skimmer in the whirl
Of heaven's whirling eye

Taniguku

Taniguku

JA

CATERPILLAR

*

Have you ever seen a caterpillar shed its skin?

*

The black larva, after eating the young leaves of the yuzu
Has grown so fat inside its skin
That his own green flesh looks translucent
He becomes still
But soon
Shudders his flanks
Between his skin and flesh
The air seeps in, and once he's sure
He begins to stretch himself
Once more, stretches as much as he can
And
                    Once more
The connection between his thorax and head tears
          It shrinks
And the caterpillar, gathering his flesh, starts to surge
This time
Tearing vertically
Swelling and peeling
          Swelling and peeling
From within the black cloak
The caterpillar reveals his green body
Its yellow-brimmed-black-dot and sky-blue stripes
A line of white dots painted around his feet—
They're beautiful
And
When three-quarters is shed
What suddenly falls
Is the black mask from his face
He puffs out his cheeks
And sweeps off his cloak through the end of his tail

*

Have you ever seen a caterpillar's chrysalis?

*

Eating yuzu leaves non-stop and crapping mountains
The speckled green caterpillar
When one size larger than a woman's pinky
Leaves the branch
And starts creeping, scurrying
To the shade, where he's protected from wind and rain
There, from his mouth
He spits out a sticky thread and glues himself down
Pulls out one strong line and
Ties it around his own body
Then stops
Sleeps where he stands
The stripes on his back
Broaden as the skin dries
He shudders
Shakes and bubbles his flanks again
Pushing at the thread
Heaving
Hauling up his flesh
            Swaying
                    Swinging
                            Careening on his lifeline
                    Becoming a humpback
            Flicking out
Horns like knives
            Hidden at the back of his neck
Cuts
His own skin
Swelling and peeling
Swelling and peeling
Then
Transforms into pure green, hard, chrysalis
Becoming a chrysalis
One of the phases of shedding

One of the phases of shedding
Have you seen it?

*

The real turning point
Took less than ten minutes
That was it

JC & RK

THE MORNING CHILD

The color of a bruise spreads across the eastern sky
The Mongolian spot of morning being born
It trembles, rustles, and wriggles upward
Crawling with all the energy of a newborn's behind
On the opposite side, the morning child regrets
Kicking open the double doors of the birth canal
It is crying about being carried
Down this river of amniotic fluid
After the afterbirth, the mother
Is an albino snake shaking her tail
Knowing there is not a trace of wind
On the seam suturing morning to night
Soothingly she sticks out her tongue
Awkwardly bends back and dives down
The path of flowers that have not bloomed
At the bottom, stamens that could not stand the sun
Suck up slippery nourishment
Now is the time they shake loose their silver pollen
The mother forgets all about the morning child
Wets her eyes and scales enough to crawl away
Then copulates with the flowers, going down the path to night
For both mother and child, the womb is the cast-off skin of a snake

The color of a bruise spreads across the eastern sky
The Mongolian spot of morning
It is the bruise on the sky which reveals
The loneliness born upon it
It trembles, rustles, and wriggles upward
With all the energy of a first attempt to crawl
No choice but to crawl upward
After swallowing to my innermost depths
The head lice mother left as a keepsake
My umbilical cord, which holds mother dangling in space
Grows thin as it turns and—oh no!—gets ready to snap
No, perhaps I'm the one left dangling upside-down
Then, the cord breaks
Mother falls into continuous night

I fall into a morning that may continue but may not—a straight line
And then
No choice but to crawl
For both mother and child, the womb is the cast-off skin of a snake

And the color of the bruise spreads
One will faintly see the blood blisters
On the morning child's hands and feet
Rip open and illuminate
The eastern sky

JA

SPECTER!

There is a girl who goes nowhere
There is a girl who sucks up severe nourishment
Like a water jug
Deep in my eyes
I illuminate
Things buried in the earth
I can see them
I can see
Gossamer shimmering illusions
Inside my body
If I close my eyes

There is a girl with roots
Could one call her lonely?
Certainly the gossamer shimmering
Under the earth does not speak
Does not touch her breasts
They simply gush
Stick up and shine, shatter into seven colors
        And that is where I sew
Like a freshwater fish
I forget myself
And travel
Still rooted
Unable to budge
I grow

How many hands
Will stick out?
Mother and father
Many mothers and fathers
Fly about and warble

I will
      Forget
           My forgotten
                  Time

If the gossamer illusions
Rise to fill the girl's fingers
Flowers will adhere to them
These first
Colors
Are what the buried ones have resigned us to

Look!
No
Close your eyes
The rustling buds
That are beginning to swell
Stroke them
        Softly
Moisten your ring finger
With a little spit

          It's running! Look,
              The specter
                  Is running
                      Through your eyes
                  Across your floor
              The girl and her gossamer illusions
      Attagirl!
Look, above your head too

"Springtime, come to us!"

JA

FOR AMENOUZUME-SAN

Open it,	that rock cave,	Amenouzume-san アメノウズメさん
Dance it,	divinely possessed,	Ameno-Vortex-Woman アメノ渦女さん
Make it rain,	heavy rain,	Ameno-Whirlpool-Eyes アメノ渦目さん
Divine it,	burning deer bones,	Ameno-Half-Open-Eyes アメノ薄目さん
Sing it,	shaking the magatama,	Ameno-Under-the-Spell アメノ有呪名さん
Weave it,	as repayment,	Ameno-Crane-Feather-Woman アメノ羽鶴女さん
Grow tall,	with Jack,	Ameno-Beanstalk アメノ芋豆芽さん
Invite them,	with her willowy hips,	Ameno-Beauty-Claws アメノ美ヅ爪さん
Run it,	the mountain ridge,	Ameno-Spurring-the-Horse アメノ打ズ馬さん
Shoot it,	her queynt,	Ameno-Shooting-Horse アメノ撃ズ馬さん
Open it,	that rock cave,	Amenouzume-san アメノウズメさん
Dance it,	your breasts out,	Ameno-Frolicking-Princess アメノ浮好姫さん
Listen to it,	distant thunder,	Ameno-Rabbit-Ears アメノ兎耳メさん
Look at it,	with pink eyes,	Ameno-Rabbit-Eyes アメノ兎ズ眼さん
Worry about it,	anguishedly,	Ameno-Anxious-and-Puzzled アメノ憂頭謎さん
Grab it,	a light grin,	Ameno-Crow-Claws アメノ烏手爪さん
Sprain it	by the ocean,	Ameno-Crouching-Woman アメノ踞女さん
Rub it,	the ninth month,	Ameno-Aching-Woman アメノ疼女さん
Push it,	one more time,	Ameno-Birth-Nest-Woman アメノ産巣女さん
It's come out,	finally,	Ameno-Baby's-Life アメノ生素命さん

Open it,	that rock cave,	Amenouzume-san アメノウズメさん
Shake it,	the heavens,	Woman-Buried-in-the-Skies 天ノ埋女さん
Make it bloom,	red cherry blossom,	Forest-Sprouts-in-the-Skies 天ノ有杜芽さん
Crawl it,	with the centipede,	Worm-in-the-Rain 雨ノ羽蚓蜈さん
Cry,	plodding on,	Riverbank-Lost-in-the-Rain 雨ノ迂洲迷さん
Lick it,	solemnly,	Drops-of-Candy 飴ノ有珠メさん
Give it,	with a whip,	Thousand-Monmes-of-Candy 飴ノ于数匁さん
Make it,	a giant mirror,	Eye-Drawing-on-the-Graph-Paper 亜眼ノ右図面さん
Tie it,	with bamboo leaves,	Knit-by-Gentle-Princess-Hands 編目ノ優手姫さん
Gather round,	multitudinous gods,	Plentiful-Rice-in-the-Skies-Witch 天ノ姥鈴米さん

Open it,	that rock cave,	Amenouzume-san アメノウズメさん
Wear it,	the magatama necklace,	Ah Clear-Agate あぁ瑪瑙澄メさん
Step on it,	roaring out,	Ah Heavy-Mortar-Ringing あぁ匁ノ臼鳴さん
Dizzy,	swooning,	That-Lightly-Wandering-Eye 或ノ眼ノ薄迷さん
In love,	half asleep,	That-Loving-Eye-Askew 或ノ愛ノズレ目さん
Bite it,	faintly,	Ah, Roots-with-Vinegar あ一芽ノ有酢メさん
Cry,	nesting,	Ah, Female-Cormorant-Residing あ一雌ノ鵜棲メさん
Whinnying,	endlessly,	Ah, Horse-All-The-Way-to-China あ一馬ノ禹州メさん
Congratulate them,	towards the east,	Ah, Heaven's-Joyous-Words 嗚呼、天ノ宇寿名さん
Calm it down,	eternal night,	Ah, Leader-of-the-Other-World 嗚呼、天ノ宇主冥さん
Take flight,	sleepy valley,	Ah, Heaven's-Guardian-of-Slumber 嗚呼、天ノ宇守暝さん

Make them laugh,	the gods,	Ah, Heaven's-Unruly-Hair-Drunks
		鳴呼、天ノ宇鬆酩さん
Good at,	stripping,	Ah, Heaven's-Thinly-Robed-Princess
		鳴呼、天ノ宇透姫さん
Take it,	the side strings,	Ah, Heaven's-Naked-Woman
		鳴呼、天ノ宇素女さん
Quaking,	it's morning,	Ah, Amenouzume-san
		鳴呼、天宇受売命さん
Shine it,	it's morning,	Ah, Amenouzume-san
		鳴呼、天宇受売命さん

Ah, Amenouzume-san
鳴呼、アメノウズメさん
Amenouzume-san
アメノウズメさん

SN

EDITOR'S AFTERWORD

Arai Takako was born in 1966 in Kiryū, a small city in central Japan that has been known for centuries for its textiles, especially the high-quality silks used to make kimono and *obi*, the highly decorated, intricately patterned, thick belts that hold kimono closed. Arai's father was the manager of a small, cottage-style weaving factory located on the family property, just next to the house where she grew up. At its height, the factory employed a few dozen people and produced some of the finely woven fabric that earned an international reputation for the region.

Many of Arai's poems focus on the lives of the women workers she saw so intimately while growing up in and around her father's factory. As Arai is quick to point out in her talks and essays, women have been traditionally associated with weaving for centuries, but when Japan started its rapid modernization in the mid-nineteenth century, the textile industry turned to women as its main source of cheap labor. Women were also most immediately affected by the collapse of the textile industry in the late twentieth and early twenty-first centuries. (Few people wear kimono day-to-day, and much production has been outsourced to developing nations where labor and materials are less expensive.) Today, Arai's family's factory continues its operations, although the pressures of globalization and the preference for other forms of clothing mean that the Arai family factory is a far smaller operation than before.

Arai came to Tokyo for her secondary education and graduated from Keiō University. She has published three books of poems to date: *The Emperor's Unfortunate Lover* (*Haō Bekki*, 1997), *Soul Dance* (*Tamashii dansu*, 2007), and *Beds and Looms* (*Betto to shokki*, 2013). Arai was one of the founders of the journal *Shimensoka* (1992-95), and later of *Mi'Te*, a quarterly journal that she continues to edit even now and that has stretched to well over one hundred and forty issues. She has served on the organizational board of the Tokyo International Poetry Festival and has a growing international reputation as one of the most exciting of Japan's younger poets, as evidenced by her appearances in poetry festivals in Argentina, Mexico, Slovenia, and the United States. In 2019, she also was a participant in the Iowa International Writing Program, which for decades has played an important role in cultivating and promoting the careers of Japanese writers abroad. Arai currently lives in Yokohama and teaches Japanese to international students at Saitama University, located to the north of the Tokyo metropolis.

Much of Arai's work is avant-garde, utilizing experimental stylistic features such as the radical juxtaposition of images, the frequent use of sentence fragments, and elements of surrealism. One characteristic of her poetry is that it, like a great deal of poetry written by younger Japanese poets, is narrative in nature. Arai is not interested in abstraction for abstraction's sake; rather, she uses poetry—sometimes in fragmentary forms, sometimes in more straightforward narrative—as a method of depicting and exploring the various ways that people engage with the world around them. Her work reminds us that in our fast-paced, eclectic society, our mental worlds are comprised of a crazy patchwork quilt of fragments of cultural elements both high and low—high-brow literature, theater, folk tales, news reports, television programs, popular music, theater, manga, and even words printed on bottles of the nutritional supplements we swallow every day. Weaving together diction borrowed from many sources, Arai consistently produces new, surprising work.

At the same time, her poems are often far more socially engaged than those of many other contemporary Japanese poets. As mentioned above, she has written a great deal about the personal and emotional ramifications of the economic decline in industrial towns like her hometown of Kiryū. In fact, the experiences of the factory workers in her writing have much in common with inhabitants of other post-industrial cities that have seen better days but continue to tough it out, such as the American Rust Belt cities of Detroit and Youngstown, or the old British industrial cities of Manchester, Newcastle, and Leeds. In particular, Arai uses her poetry to keep the memory of the women workers she saw during her youth alive, even as the factories where they once worked are quickly turning into vacant lots. For instance, in the poems "When the Moon Rises" and "Bobbins," she describes the ways that gestures learned in textile factories remain part of women's lives, even long after the factories themselves have closed down. Similarly, in "Colored Glass," she imagines the ways that the factory gets into the worker's soul in even more literal terms—this surreal poem describes a girl swallowing a silkworm so that her body itself becomes the factory where silk is produced. In "Beds and Looms," the title poem from her third and arguably most important book of poetry to date, Arai describes the ways that the personal, sexual lives of the women workers intersect with life on the factory floor. Other poems have explored the ways women's lives have been shaped by contemporary trends, including the push toward globalization and the economic downturn in the first decade of the twenty-first century. For instance, the poem "Clusters of Falling Stars," is a poem of protest inspired by Horie Takafumi, the CEO of an IT company who engaged in securities fraud and caused widespread economic harm. In her poem, Arai focuses on how Horie's malfeasance affected ordinary people, even those who had little direct connection to him.

Like many poets throughout Japan, Arai felt the call to respond through poetry to the catastrophic 2011 earthquake, tsunami, and nuclear meltdown in northeastern Japan. In fact, Arai was a frequent participant in the many poetry vigils held in Japan throughout 2011 to raise money for the victims of the disasters. Her poem "Galapagos," written soon after the earthquake, is one of the rare poems that uses humor to explore the ongoing issues that caused and have arisen from the disasters. In this poem, Arai takes many of the issues in the Japanese press in the following year and synthesized them into an organic whole—the ongoing anxiety about the Japanese economy during the ongoing Fukushima crisis, concern about the extremely low national birthrate, concern that people in the directly affected regions should not be having sex for fear of abnormalities, and even worries about the lack of individuality of Japanese youth as manifested in the almost universal tendency to wear clothes from Uniqlo (an inexpensive clothing store known for its simple, cool fashions). In fact, in the wake of so much bad news in 2011, Uniqlo's entry into several new, major global markets in 2012 was a ray of hope to the Japanese media, which seized upon it as a step forward for business and the economy. Given this publicity, it is perhaps no surprise Arai singles out Uniqlo for particular attention.

The poem "Half a Pair of Shoes," was inspired by a trip Arai made in the immediate aftermath of the 2011 disasters to Kesennuma, one of the coastal cities almost completely washed away by the tsunami. At the time of her visit, the shoes and clothing of the victims and other coastal inhabitants were still lying on the shore, washed there by the waves. The sight of a single shoe on the sand and rocks becomes the starting point for this poem exploring what it means to be a writer attempting to reconstruct the stories of victims based on physical evidence alone. The poem "Lots and Lots" was inspired by the commentary of several authors writing post-Fukushima about the ways that the Japanese population had become desensitized to the idea of atomic power, even though their experiences with atomic energy in Hiroshima and Nagasaki had been nothing short of nightmarish. She singles out the work of the manga artist Tezuka Osamu (1928-1989), whose wildly popular comic character "Iron-Armed Atom" (*Tetsuwan Atomu*) suggested to the Japanese population that nuclear power could be used for good. As Arai points out in the first stanza, the character's name was changed to "Astro Boy" when the animated feature based on this comic was first exported to the United States. Throughout this poem, Arai uses Tezuka's character "Atom" as a stand-in for the fifty-four nuclear stations located throughout Japan. The final stanzas riff on three classic modern Japanese poems: Yoshioka Minoru's "Monks" (*Sōryo*), Anzai Fuyue's "Spring" (*Haru*), and Hagiwara Sakutarō's "Bamboo and Its Grief" (*Take to sono aishō*). By ironically and humorously rewriting these famous poems in ways that are relevant to the Fukushima meltdown, Arai shows the ways that the power of poetry—even poems already in existence—can be harnessed and rewritten to produce commentary in a time of crisis.

The 2011 disasters were, in fact, a turning point in Arai's career. With the support of the Museum of Contemporary Japanese Poetry, Tanka and Haiku, located in the far north of Japan, she began to repeatedly visit temporary housing facilities in the earthquake and tsunami-ravaged coastal town of Ōfunato, where she worked with residents to express themselves through poetry. There, far from the poetry scene of Tokyo, she discovered a small, local poetry scene with several talented figures whom Arai worked to bring to greater national attention. During her repeated trips to the northeast, Arai became obsessed with the colorful and expressive local language, known as *Kesengo*, which over the course of the last century, had been slowly supplanted and suppressed by *Hyōjungo*, the standardized Japanese language used in education, literature, film, and television. Together with her Ōfunato friends, most of whom were elderly women, she worked to translate the works of the famous modern tanka poet Ishikawa Takuboku (1886-1912) from Hyōjungo into Kesengo. Takuboku had come from the region but, like most poets, wrote not in his native dialect but in a combination of classical and standardized modern Japanese. This unusual translation project helped the local poets to reclaim, valorize, and record their own language, which had been shunted to the sidelines in the development of modern literature. The resulting book, *Songs of Takuboku: Translations by the Old Women of the Northeast* (*Takuboku no uta: Tōhoku onba-yaku*), was praised in the press for reevaluating the language and cultural contributions of northeastern Japan, a place that many other regions of modern Japan have derided as being culturally and developmentally behind.

Her experiences in the northeast reaffirmed for Arai the importance of local language and dialect in shaping identity and self-expression. For many years, Arai had been an avid fan of the work of the experimental playwright Kara Jūrō, who uses long, colloquial speeches and surreal, almost magic-realist plots to explore the lives of commoners, especially the poor and working-class people living at the margins of society. Learning from Kara, Arai had included in *Soul Dance* a number of soliloquy-like poems in dialect about the factory girls of her hometown. In *Beds and Looms*, published two years after Arai began traveling to the northeast, she used even more dialect—sometimes that of her own region, sometimes that of the northeast—to channel the voices of people living at the margins.

Although standardized Japanese has been the dominant language for most modern and contemporary poetry, Arai recognizes there are certain feelings and ideas that can only be expressed in the down-to-earth, highly individualistic, colloquial language used in day-to-day life. Carol Hayes and Rina Kikuchi, who contributed some of the translations in this book, have characterized Arai's poems in dialect as being composed of "imagined language." Within any particular dialect, there are significant individual variations between speakers of different ages, social classes, and genders, thus making it necessary for Arai to imagine and develop a particular style of speech for each narrator to use. Needless to say, the specific textures and qualities of these dialectical choices are difficult to reproduce in translation, especially considering that the most noticeable variations in English dialects come in pronunciation, which is difficult to represent on the page.

Considering how much Arai loves the theater and how much attention she pays to the voice, it is perhaps no surprise that when she reads her own work, she is an outstanding performer. Most contemporary Japanese poetry is written for the page, and poetry readings are somewhat less common in Japan than in the English-speaking world. As a result, there are relatively few poets who can electrify an audience solely with their voice. Arai, however, is one of the rare exceptions. Within the space of just a few moments, she transforms the space around her. As the pitch of her voice rises and falls, weaving in and out of dialect and modulating between quiet whispers and impassioned cries, she captivates her audiences, channeling voices as if through some shamanic ritual. It is the sincerest hope of the editor that in the book you now hold in your hands, you will discover some of the drama and raw, visceral power of Arai's poetry.

—Jeffrey Angles
Kalamazoo, 2019

NOTES ON THE TRANSLATIONS

Except for on the cover of this book, where the author's name appears for the sake of cataloguing in the English order (with given name followed by family name), the remainder of this book follows the increasingly common practice of keeping East Asian names in the order used in the region: family name followed by given name. In other words, when people speak in Japanese about the poet represented here, she is referred to as Arai Takako.

The initials that appear after each poem refer to that poem's translators:

JA = Jeffrey Angles
JC = Jen Crawford
CH = Carol Hayes
RK= Rina Kikuchi
YN = You Nakai
SN = Sawako Nakayasu

Wheels: It is common in many Japanese families, especially religious ones, to have a Buddhist altar in the home. There one finds images of Buddhist deities, candlesticks, offerings, memorial tablets, and photos of deceased relatives.

Beds and Looms: -*Chan* is a diminutive suffix used after a person's name or sometimes just the first-syllable of a person's name (or perhaps beloved pet animal's name) in order to show affection. -*Yan* is another diminutive suffix, used in Gunma dialect, to attach to a name, usually that of a man. The remainder of the poem contains a number of references to Japanese Buddhist culture. In Japan, Buddhist priests typically wear beautifully woven, ornately patterned robes requiring a high level of skill, and the town of Kiryū from which Arai comes, was known for producing them. The River of the Three Hells is the river separating the world of the living from the world of the dead in Buddhist mythology. The reference to Maria-Kannon comes from the premodern era, when Christianity was prohibited in Japan. During that time, a small minority of "hidden Christians" clung to their beliefs and secretly used Buddhist images to practice their beliefs. For instance, they used the image of Kannon, the Buddhist goddess of mercy, as an image of the Christ's mother Mary. The words "secret buddha" *(hibutsu)* are a euphemism for a woman's genitals. "Form itself is emptiness, Emptiness itself is form" is a line from the

Heart Sutra, one of the most commonly recited Buddhist texts.

Nylon Scarf: As mentioned in the previous note, it is common in Japan to take the first part of a person's name and add the diminutive suffix *-chan* to show affection toward them. The narrator of the poem only ever used a diminutive to refer to the older girl, so that is why she cannot remember her complete name. Scooping up goldfish with thin paper nets is a common game at Japanese festivals. People can take home as many goldfish as they can scoop up before the paper net breaks apart.

The Healds: A heald frame is part of a weaving loom. The frame works to separate and lift some of the warp yarns above others, thus allowing the shuttle to pass through, holding the weft. Heald frames are rectangular and are supported by a set of thin wires called "healds" or "hettles." Healds are attached to the frame vertically, and the threads move through their eyeholes while weaving. A "magic lantern" (*gentō*) is something like an early slide projector, first developed in the seventeenth century, and directs light through small, rectangular slides onto a wall or screen. The word *kamaitachi* ("whirlwind") describes the cutting turbulent winds common in Japan's northern snow country. Traditional folk tales tell of weasel-like creatures that fly on whirlwinds slashing at human skin. In this poem, the focus is on the wind rather than this mythological creature. *Banzai* roughly translates as "hurray" or "long life," and when people say it, they often raise their arms over their heads. A warp beam is part of a loom. The ends of the warp threads are wound onto a warp beam roller at the back of the loom. A coiffeur *(kamiyui)* is someone who works as a hair dresser or barber, maintaining the complex hairdos women wore in traditional Japan.

Green Wings: A beater is the part of the loom that a weaver pulls down quickly and firmly to press the weft into place. In Japan, it is said that cicadas live in the ground for seven years before emerging. When cicadas take off into flight, they often expel urine to surprise potential predators. In this poem, the finger-turned-cicada hopes Kiyoko will notice it and recognize her own scent.

Masae: This poem is set during World War II, when many Japanese soldiers were conscripted and shipped out, never to return again. Luzon, the Filipino island where the army sent the main character's son, was the site of an eight-month-long battle that claimed the lives of approximately 200,000 Japanese soldiers through injury, starvation, and illness. Sashimi are slices of raw fish, often eaten with soy sauce and wasabi horseradish. (Sashimi should not be confused with sushi, which is something—usually raw fish or pickled vegetables—served on top of or rolled up with vinegar-flavored rice.) A *suikinkutsu* is a musical water feature sometimes found in traditional Japanese gardens. Water drips into a ceramic jar half-filled with water, making a metallic plinking sound that reverberates and amplifies inside the jar.

Flared Skirt: *Buchi* refers to splotches of color and is therefore a common name for a tabby cat. A *kotatsu* is a low square-shaped Japanese style table that is used as a heater. A tabletop sits on top of a quilt, which is placed over the *kotatsu* frame while a heater underneath warms the enclosed space underneath the table. The phrase "*eeeek-mew eeeek-mew*" is an English approximation of Arai's own original onomatopoeia *chiimyaa, chiimyaa*, which combines the squeaking of a mouse with the mewing of a kitten. While a number of Japanese foods are now commonly known in English, red bean rice *(sekihan)* is less familiar. In this dish, small red azuki beans are cooked with white rice to celebrate special occasions since the color red is associated with happy occasions in Japan. This dish was commonly made by households to share with neighbours on the birth of a child or a marriage so neighbors could symbolically share in the happiness. A *hanten* is a short, padded jacket that is worn over kimono, pyjamas, or other clothes at home. Like "*eeeek-mew eeeek-mew*" above, the phrase *ogyaua-aan* (here translated as "*waaah—meioooowww*") was also invented by Arai, combining the cry of a wailing baby and the yowl of a cat on heat. This example also demonstrates one of the characteristics of Arai's "imagined" language, her distinctive use of katakana within a single word or phrase. In traditional, Japanese-style houses, rooms with *tatami* (straw-mat flooring) are where one usually finds the family Buddhist altar with memorial tablets for deceased relatives.

Colored Glass: The poem reflects the collapse of the silk and textile industry in Arai's hometown of Kiryū. In this poem, she imagines a person swallowing a silkworm, which begins to grow and create its own silk factory inside her stomach. The poem was inspired by the Japanese expression *Nigamushi o kamitubusu* (literally, "to squash a bitter bug in your teeth"), which is used to describe someone's expression as they frown or grimace. Many of the textile factories in Kiryū had roofs that zigzag up and down like the teeth on a saw, hence the phrase "sawtooth roof" *(nokogiri-yane)* in the poem. Glass windows would then be placed on one side of each "tooth" of the roof to let in light. In the final stanza, Arai imagines a mini-silk factory floating in the narrator's stomach, the colored glass in the sawtooth roof illuminating the interior. The lines "roll your hands, round and round, pull your eyes flat" *(kaiguri kaiguri* *totto no me*) are from a children's game. The child rolls their hands around one another as if they are rolling up thread on their hands like a spinning wheel, then after that, they pull at the corner of their eyes. Arai creates a variation on this song, imagining that the narrator pulls her own eyes out.

Clusters of Falling Stars: In this poem, Arai refers to the collapse of the textile industry as well as the arrest of the young CEO and television personality Horie Takafumi. Horie's company Livedoor had bought up massive amounts of stock in media-related companies, so when he was arrested for securities fraud in 2006, it became a national media event. Tanabata, sometimes called the "Star Festival" in English, is held during the summer on July 7. On that day, people write their wishes on long cards and hang them on a spring of bamboo.

Give Us Morning: This poem was written at the time of the Iraq War and the 2004 tsunami in the Indian Ocean. In an interview for the journal *Full Tilt,* Arai commented, "Every morning, I would wake up, turn on the TV or open the newspaper only to find reports of the numbers of the dead… It seems so ironic to see such terrible tragedies and cruelty transposed into numbers. At the same time, I wanted to try to depict the mornings that surrounded those huge and weighty numbers." Amenouzume is a mythical Japanese goddess associated with dance and performance. Through her dance, she is said to have lured the Sun Goddess Amaterasu out of a rock cave where she had secluded herself, thus plunging the world into darkness. The words "womanly shadow" that appear toward the end of the poem is a euphemism for the vagina.

Come, Come, Fall Fast Asleep: The title phrase "come, come, fall fast asleep" (*nen-nen korori yo*) comes from a well-known Japanese lullaby. This poem was published in a major Japanese newspaper some months after the Fukushima meltdown when diagrams of the nuclear reactors were still appearing in the news on an almost daily basis.

Galapagos: Like the previous poem, this was written after the 2011 disasters in northeastern Japan. The title comes from the fact that commentators on the Japanese economy sometimes compare Japan to the Galapagos, the isolated group of Ecuadorian islands where developments frequently veer off in their own unique directions, different from those of the rest of the world. This poem also comments on serious issues—the ongoing anxiety about the Japanese economy during the nuclear crisis in Fukushima, concern about the extremely low national birthrate, and even the lack of individuality of Japanese youth. In referring to the low national birth rate, Arai jokes that Japan does not have much "fusion" of sperm and ova; instead what the Japanese population has is mostly "fission"—the breaking apart of radioactive isotopes as seen in the Fukushima meltdown. In this work, Arai pokes fun at the discriminatory idea, circulated in the popular media and on blogs, that young people from the polluted areas ought to consider using condoms rather than having unprotected sex for fear that radiation might have had long-term, unpredictable effects on them and their progeny. In commenting on this poem, Arai has mentioned that she wanted to show that the tendency in Japan to put economics first led not only to the nuclear accident; it also has brought people to a point where they feel compelled to limit their own freedoms and joy. In the middle of the poem, Arai lines up a number of words that all end with the syllable *bō*. As she watched the press coverage of the Fukushima meltdown, she was surprised that so many of the items filling the news ended with the same sound.

Half a Pair of Shoes: This poem was inspired by a trip Arai made in the immediate aftermath of the 2011 disasters to Kesennuma, one of the coastal cities almost completely washed away by the tsunami. At the time of her visit, the shoes and clothing of the victims and other coastal inhabitants were still washing onto the shore. The sight of a single shoe lying on the shore becomes the starting point for this poem exploring what it means to be a poet attempting to reconstruct the stories of victims based on physical evidence alone.

Lots and Lots: This poem was inspired by the books *This is How We Chose to Be a "Nuclear Power" (Watashi-tachi wa kōshite "genpatsu ōkoku" o eranda)* by Takeda Tōru and *The Atomic Energy We Dreamed of (Yume no genshiryoku)* by Yoshimi Shun'ya. Both books talk about the ways in which the Japanese population was desensitized to the idea of atomic power in the postwar period, even though Japan's experiences with atomic weaponry at Hiroshima and Nagasaki had been nothing short of nightmarish. Takeda points to the role of the popular manga artist Tezuka Osamu (1928-1989), whose wildly popular comic character "Iron-Armed Atom" *(Tetsuwan Atomu)* suggested to the Japanese population that nuclear power could be used for good. As Arai points out in the first stanza, the character's name was changed to "Astro Boy" when the animated feature based on this comic was first exported to the United States. Meanwhile, Atom's little sister is named "Uran" (from the word "Uranium") and his younger brother "Cobalt." Throughout this poem,

Arai uses Tezuka's character "Atom" as a stand-in for the fifty-four nuclear stations located throughout Japan. Regarding the names that Arai mentions in the first stanza, Tsutomu means "strong" or "dedicated," while Isamu means "brave." Both names were popular during the 1950s when the manga artist Tezuka Osamu was at work on Astro Boy. Professor Ochanomizu and Dr. Tenma are characters that appear in Tezuka's manga. In the fourth stanza, Arai suggests that in the male-dominated era of the 1950s, Tezuka did not want to create a female robot. To avoid gender confusion, he used the English word "Atom" to name his character instead of using the Japanese equivalent. The reason is that the word meaning "atom" in Japanese is written 原子 *(genshi)*, but since the character 子 *(ko)* appears at the end of many girls' names in contemporary Japan, this name might lead readers to assume the character was female. The final stanzas riff on three classic modern Japanese poems: Yoshioka Minoru's "Monks" (Sōryo), Anzai Fuyue's "Spring" (Haru), and Hagiwara Sakutarō's "Bamboo and its Grief" (Take to sono aishō). By ironically and humorous rewriting these famous poems in ways that are relevant to the Fukushima meltdown, Arai shows the ways that the power of poetry—even poems already in existence—can be harnessed and rewritten to produce commentary in a time of crisis.

Eh-janaika, Eh-janaika: For a brief time in the late 1860s (at the end of the Edo period), a fanatical dance called "Eh-janaika" spread in various parts of Japan. It was conducted by the masses, especially believers of the Ise faith. While playing the taiko drums and shamisen, the words *Eh-janaika* were chanted in time with dance steps, and this phrase has since come to describe the entire movement. Commoners who were struggling financially would, as a group, barge into the homes of their village headman, eat and drink his alcohol, steal his money and goods, all while singing and dancing in a festive manner. This served to undermine and overthrow their hierarchical relationship, as well as that between lender and borrower. These acts of revolt are also seen as representing ideals of social reform. The Kantō district refers to the eastern central region of Japan, with Tokyo as its core. The Kansai district refers to a western central region of Japan, surrounding Kyoto and Osaka. Mino and Mikawa are areas that lie between Kantō and Kansai. Tsugaru jongara music is rhythmical, traditional music from Aomori Prefecture, in far northern Japan. The shamisen is a banjo-like traditional instrument with a long neck and three strings. In the south of Japan (Okinawa Prefecture, for example), snake-skin is used for making the instrument. A taiko is a traditional Japanese drum. Japonesia is a term coined by the novelist Shimao Toshio, referring to a cultural region linking Japanese islands with many islands in the East China Sea, regardless of national boundaries. The Shōwa period lasted from 1926 to 1989 CE. Ippen was a monk who was active in the 13th century. In his efforts to spread Buddhism to the people, he began a dancing form of chanting, where he danced to the words *Namu Amida Butsu*, a phrase that came from Sanskrit through Chinese into Japanese and that means something like "All Praise to the Buddha Amitabha."

Supplements: Food supplements have long been popular in Japan, even before the newest wave of supplements popular in the West reached its shores. Throughout the poem, Arai tends to associate names of supplements that have lots of alliteration in the Japanese, but the translations do not always line up quite as neatly as the Japanese. For instance, in the second line she lines up lipoic acid (*riposan*) next to malic acid (*ringosan*), both of which start and end with the same sounds. *Hohokekyo* and *kekyo* are onomatopoeias that represent the sound of a nightingale singing. The names of the supplements are written in combination of the two syllabaries of Japanese, the katakana syllabary used for borrowed words and plant names, as well as the hiragana syllabary used for indigenous worlds. In the second stanza, she lists supplements that are written in long strings of kanji (Sino-Chinese characters). These have been included in italics to give a sense of how different they look from the rest of the poem. As the kanji compounds grow more complex, they degenerate into amusing nonsense. In fact, the last six names are medicines that Arai made up entirely.

Soul Dance: The word "Disaster-day" that Arai has invented in this bizarre and humorous poem is a homonym for the word meaning "Tuesday" *(kayōbi)*. The invented word "Drunk-day" is a homonym for the word meaning "Wednesday" (*suiyōbi*).

Existence: The italicized lines at the beginning of the text come from a common Japanese children's game. Two teams line up, taking sides. One side chants the lines, pretending to offer a bunch of flowers to the other team for one of their players, then the two teams play paper-scissors-rock to see which member of the other team comes over to their side. (In Japanese, these lines read, "*Dono ko ga hoshii hana ichi-monme / Ano ko ga hoshii hana ichi-monme.*" Arai specifically requested that the word *ko* meaning "child" be translated here as "girl.") A *monme* is an old unit of measurement worth 3.75 grams; here, "One monme's worth of flowers" refers to the quantity of flowers 3.75 grams of silver could purchase. In the second italicized passage, Arai has playfully modified the usual lines, which ordinarily go, "We're miserable s/he lost, one monme's worth of flowers" (*Makete kuyashii hana ichi-monme*). The words "lose" (*makete*) and "mock" or "parody" (*magete*) that Arai uses in these lines are near homonyms in Japanese and reflect an association through sound. Pachinko is a Japanese game somewhat like pinball played with many balls at the same time. When one does well, the game starts spitting out more balls for the player to reuse or to exchange for prizes or money. Here, the image of sperm jumping from their dish is compared to pachinko machines spitting out balls. In pachinko parlors, one often hears marches playing over the loudspeakers, hence the mention of marches so soon before the mention of pachinko.

Mohei's Fire: Some of the distances described in old Japanese units of measurement in this poem have been converted into feet and yards, the phrase "two *ken*" was translated as "four yards", and "nine *shaku*" as "nine feet." The Inari shrine is said to have a fox as its messenger, thus the common food item, Inari-zushi, made with fried tofu wrapped around vinegar-flavored rice, is derived from the idea that foxes love oily foods. Shinobazu-no-ike pond is located in Ueno, one of the centers of downtown Tokyo. The Shōwa period lasted from 1926 until 1989, and so the "early Shōwa period" usually refers to the years from the latter half of 1920s into the 1930s.

The Taniguku: *Taniguku* is an archaic Japanese word for a toad. The final sound "*guku*" appears to have come from an onomatopoeia representing the sound of a toad croaking. The expression "lower mouth" is a euphemism for the vagina.

The Morning Child: Children in many East Asian countries are often born with a large bluish spot on their backsides known as a Mongolian spot. In almost all cases, the spot fades away by the time the child turns seven or eight years old.

For Amenouzume-san: As mentioned above in the notes for "Give Us Morning," Amenouzume is a mythical Japanese goddess associated with dance and performance. Through her dance, she is said to have lured the Sun Goddess Amaterasu out of a rock cave where she had secluded herself, thus plunging the world into darkness. Through her dance, Amenouzume managed to restore the world to light. In modern Japanese orthography, the names of gods are often written phonetically, but in this poem, Arai playfully substitutes a wide variety of characters that are homophones or near-homophones for the various parts of her name to produce lighthearted, even humorous results. For instance, in the second line she inserts into the name usually written アメノウズメさん (*Amenouzume-san*), two characters meaning "vortex (渦, read *uzu*) and "woman" (女, read *me*) to get アメノ 渦女さん (pronounced *Amenouzume-san*, but meaning "Ameno-Vortex-Woman" as it is translated literally here). *Magatama* are curved beads which were often found in graves, as offerings to deities. They were also popularly worn as jewels for decoration since their physical shape was believed represent the human spirit. In Japanese, "giving candy while cracking the whip" is a well-known idiom, in which one leads another with both indulgence and strictness, finding its parallel in the English idiom, "carrot and stick." As mentioned above in the note for the poem "Existence," a *monme* is an old unit of measurement equivalent to about 3.75 grams.

ORIGINAL TITLES AND SOURCES OF POEMS

From *Soul Dance* 『タマシイ・ダンス』(2007)
- Backyard 「裏庭」
- Bobbins 「糸車」
- Clusters of Falling Stars 「流星群」
- Colored Glass 「色硝子」
- Eh-Janaika, Eh-Janaika 「えぇじゃないか、えぇじゃないか」
- For Amenouzume 「アメノウズメ賛江」
- Give Us Morning 「朝をください」
- Soul Dance 「タマシイ・ダンス」
- Supplements 「サプリ」
- The Morning Child 「朝の子」
- The Taniguku 「谷蟆」
- Wheels 「Wheels」
- When the Moon Rises 「月が昇ると、」

From *Beds and Looms* 『ベットと織機』(2013)
- Beds and Looms 「ベットと織機」
- Come, Come, Fall Fast Asleep 「ねんねんころりよ」
- Flared Skirt 「フレアスカート」
- Galapagos 「ガラパゴス」
- Green Wings 「みどりの翅」
- Half a Pair of Shoes 「片方の靴」
- The Healds 「ヘルド」
- Lots and Lots 「わんさ、わんさと」
- Masae 「まさ江」
- Nylon Scarf 「ナイロンスカーフ」
- Specter! 「スペクトル！」

Uncollected Poems
- Existence 「実存」 *Mi'Te*, vol.146 (2019)
- Membrane 「ホルモン」 *Mi'Te*, vol. 126 (2014)
- Mohei's Fire 「茂兵衛の火」 *Mi'Te*, vol. 88 (2006)
- Shadows 「翳たち」 *Bungakukai* (July 2008)

The translators would like to thank the editors of the various literary journals and anthologies in which these translations originally appeared.

BIOGRAPHIES

Takako Arai is an avant-garde poet born in 1966 in Kiryū, Japan, an area historically known for its magnificent weaving. She is the author of three Japanese books of poetry, and is known for her descriptions of lives of the women she saw in the small factory on her father's property. She is the winner of the Oguma Hideo Prize and was a participant in the Iowa International Writing Program. She lives in Yokohama and is an associate professor at Saitama University.

Jeffrey Angles is a bilingual poet working in both Japanese and English. His book of Japanese poetry *Watashi no hizuke henkōsen* (My International Date Line, 2016) won the Yomiuri Prize for Literature, making him the first non-native speaker ever to win this prestigious prize for poetry. His many translations include *Killing Kanoko* by Hiromi Itō (Action Books, 2009) and the modernist classic *The Book of the Dead* by Shinobu Orikuchi (University of Minnesota Press, 2016). He is a professor of Japanese literature at Western Michigan University.

Jen Crawford is an assistant professor of Writing within the Centre for Creative and Cultural Research at the University of Canberra. Her critical writing focuses on the poetics of place and on cross-cultural engagements in various literary contexts. She is the author of eight poetry books and chapbooks, including *Koel* (Cordite Books, 2016), and co-editor of *Poet to Poet: Contemporary Women Poets from Japan* (Recent Work Press, 2017) with Rina Kikuchi.

Carol Hayes is a professor of Japanese language and literature at the Australian National University. Her research interests include Japanese cultural production with a focus on modern Japanese literature and poetry and Japanese-language teaching. Her recent publications include the edited volume *Japan in Australia* (with David Chapman, Routledge, 2019), a volume of bilingual poetry *Dark-Fire-Sutra: Yami no hi to kyō* (with Noriko Tanaka, Miotsukushi, 2019) and *Baba Akiko: Intabyū* (Tanka Kenkyū, 2018).

Rina Kikuchi is a poetry scholar and the editor/translator of two bilingual poetry anthologies: *Poet to Poet: Contemporary Women Poets from Japan* (Recent Work Press, 2017) with Jen Crawford and *Pleasant Troubles* (Recent Work Press, 2018) with Harumi Kawaguchi. She is currently an associate professor at Shiga University and an adjunct associate professor at the University of Canberra.

You Nakai conducts research on experimental/electronic music, post-dance, history of tablatures, the occult mechanism of influence and other curiosities. He earned a Ph.D. from New York University and is the author of *Reminded by the Instruments: David Tudor's Music* (Oxford University Press, forthcoming). You also produces music(ians), dance(rs), picture books, ghost houses and other forms of work as part of No Collective and organizes the experimental publishing project Already Not Yet in Brooklyn.

Sawako Nakayasu is an artist working with language, performance, and translation. Her books include *Texture Notes* (Letter Machine Editions, 2010), *The Ants* (Les Figues Press, 2014), and *Some Girls Walk into the Country They Are From* (Wave Books, forthcoming). Her translations include *The Collected Poems of Chika Sagawa* (Canarium Books, 2015), and *Mouth: Eats Color— Sagawa Chika Translations, Anti-translations, & Originals* (Rogue Factorial, 2011), a multilingual work of both original and translated poetry. She teaches at Brown University.